D0492708

THE
LINGERING CRISIS
OF YOUTH
UNEMPLOYMENT

by

ARVIL V. ADAMS and GARTH L. MANGUM

with

Wayne Stevenson
Stephen F. Seninger
Stephen L. Mangum

June 1978

THE W. E. UPJOHN INSTITUTE FOR EMPLOYMENT RESEARCH

Library of Congress Cataloging in Publication Data

Adams, Arvil V
    The lingering crisis of youth unemployment.

    Bibliography: p.
    1. Youth--Employment--United States. 2. Unemployed
--United States. I. Mangum, Garth L., joint author.
II. Upjohn Institute for Employment Research. III. Title.
HD6273.A64   331.3'4'0973   78-16706

THE BOARD OF TRUSTEES OF THE
W.E. UPJOHN UNEMPLOYMENT TRUSTEE CORPORATION

THE STAFF OF THE INSTITUTE

To

Bennye, Gregory, Christopher, and Cynthia

FOREWORD

The severity of youth unemployment in the United States has received considerable attention at the national level during recent months. According to the U.S. Department of Labor, in the fourth quarter of 1977 the seasonally adjusted unemployment rate for youths 16 to 19 years old was 16.7 percent, and for nonwhite youth the jobless rate was 38.3 percent. These rates are about two and one-half times greater than the jobless rates for the total labor force and for the total nonwhite segment of the labor force.

In this reassessment of the youth unemployment problem, the authors have sought to establish the dimensions of youth unemployment and its underlying causes and consequences, to determine the priorities that should be attached to the problem, and to suggest policies that would lead toward its solution. The implications of changing population and occupational structures should provide important guidelines for government officials, educators, employers, and manpower planners regarding policy decisions that will be required during the next decade if continued high levels of unemployment for youth, particularly for black youths, are to be avoided.

Facts and observations expressed in the study are the sole responsibility of the authors. Their viewpoints do not necessarily represent positions of the W. E. Upjohn Institute for Employment Research or of the U.S. Department of Labor.

E. Earl Wright
Director

Kalamazoo, Michigan
June 1978

THE AUTHORS

Arvil V. Adams is professor of economics and associate director of the Human Resources Institute, the University of Utah. He is currently on leave serving as executive director of the National Commission on Employment and Unemployment Statistics. He formerly held academic appointments at The Ohio State University and the University of Kentucky. He is the author or coauthor of thirty or more monographs and articles. His most recent publications include: *Earnings and Employment of Middle-Aged Men: A Special Study of Their Investment in Human Capital; Interregional Migration, Education, and Poverty in the Urban Ghetto: Another Look at Black-White Earnings Differentials; The Stock of Human Capital;* and *Differences in Post-School Formal Occupational Training for Middle-Aged Men.*

Garth L. Mangum holds the McGraw Chair in economics and management at the University of Utah and is director of the Human Resources Institute at that school. He is a member and former chairman of the National Council on Economic Policy. He was staff director of the Senate Subcommittee on Employment and Manpower as well as executive director of the President's Commission on Manpower during the formative years of the 1960s. Dr. Mangum is author or coauthor of more than 20 books and of 100 articles and monographs. His most recent publications include: *Employability, Employment and Income; A Decade of Manpower Development and Training; Metropolitan Impact on Manpower Programs; Human Resources and Labor Markets;* and *Manpower Planning for Local Labor Markets.*

Wayne Stevenson is assistant professor of economics at the University of Utah. Since receiving his Ph.D. from the University of Minnesota in 1972, he has taught extensively in the area of human resources management. His main interest is in quantitative analysis and he has written a text on empirical methods for human resources research. Other research activities and publications are in the area of labor market analysis.

Stephen F. Seninger is a research associate professor of economics and associate director of the Human Resources Institute at the University of Utah. He received his Ph.D. degree from Washington University and has been involved with teaching and research in the areas of urban/regional economics and government expenditure analysis.

Stephen Mangum is a graduate student in Human Resource Management at the University of Utah.

PREFACE

High unemployment among American youth, especially among black youth, has become a critical manpower problem. Unemployment among 16 to 24 year olds reached record levels in the mid-1970s, accounting for nearly one of every two unemployed Americans. By comparison, this population accounted for only one out of five of those employed. With increased public concern generated by these high levels of youth unemployment has come the need to reexamine the problem, its causes and consequences, to determine what priority should be assigned it and what policies are appropriate to its solution.

This study, a reassessment of the youth unemployment problem, was prepared through the Human Resources Institute of the University of Utah, with a grant from the W. E. Upjohn Institute for Employment Research, Kalamazoo, Michigan. Additional support was received from the Institutional Grant Program of the Office of Research and Development, the U.S. Department of Labor, Employment and Training Administration.

The study is based on analysis of recent trends in youth unemployment from published sources and on additional analysis of a national sample of young men and young women 16 to 19 years of age who were followed longitudinally over a seven-year period in the late 1960s and early 1970s. Among the most significant findings are: (1) joblessness among out-of-school teenage youth carries with it a "hangover" effect. Those who have unfavorable early labor market experiences are less likely than others to have favorable subsequent experiences, education and other background characteristics held constant, and (2) education and training have a significant positive effect upon the employment and earnings of youth by race and sex.

No study of this size can be prepared without the creative and logistical support of many individuals. Our debts are many. We would like to acknowledge the assistance of Mary Patterson in programming and data analysis. Steve Rich, Rex Fuller, and Dayle Nattress made significant contributions as research assistants. Numerous drafts of the manuscript were cheerfully typed by Gwen Luke and Ivis Steele, and Sybil Clays prepared the manuscript for publication. Readers of earlier drafts who provided constructive comments and suggestions included Glen Cain, Alan Gustman, George Iden, Edward Kalachek, Sar Levitan, Herbert Parnes, Ellen Sehgal, and Gregory Wurzburg. To all we express our appreciation. We alone, however, are responsible for the contents.

Arvil V. Adams
Garth L. Mangum

CONTENTS

Foreword   vi

Preface   ix

Chapter One   The Nature of Youth Unemployment   1
Arvil V. Adams, Garth L. Mangum,
and Stephen F. Seninger

Expanding Youth Population   4
Growth of Aggregate Demand   5
Labor Market Barriers to Youth   7
Urbanization and Minority Employment   8
Transition From School to Work   10
Notes   13

Chapter Two   Postwar Trends in Youth Unemployment .   19
Stephen F. Seninger

The Postwar Baby Boom   19
Black Compared with White Youth
Unemployment   24
Occupation and Industry Trends   26
Changes in Economic Activity   26
Other Postwar Trends   30
Policy Response   31
Notes   34

xi

Chapter Three   A Look at Youth Unemployment in the
                 Mid-1970s 35
                 Arvil V. Adams and
                 Wayne Stevenson

                 Population and Labor Force
                 Participation 36
                    Young Employed 38
                    Young Unemployed 38
                 Reviewing the Evidence 48
                 Notes 49

Chapter Four   A Changing Economy and Its Effect
                 Upon Youth Unemployment
                 in the Eighties 51
                 Stephen Mangum and
                 Arvil V. Adams

                 Employment and Labor Force
                 Projections 53
                 Youth Unemployment Projections 58
                 Prospects for Youth Employment 62

Chapter Five   The Transition From School to Work ... 65
                 Wayne Stevenson

                 Approach to the Problem 66
                 School Enrollment and Labor Force
                 Participation 67
                    Entry-Level Jobs............... 70
                 Early Labor Market Success 76
                 Correlates of Early
                 Labor Market Experience 79
                 Labor Force Participation
                 and Unemployment 81
                 Wages, Weeks Worked, and
                 Annual Earnings 84
                 Conclusions 90
                 Notes 90

Chapter Six   The Relationship Between Early Work
                     Experience and Future Employability   93
                         Wayne Stevenson

                         Changing Employment Patterns   94
                         Wages, Weeks Worked, and
                         Annual Earnings   99
                         Early Labor Market Experience
                         and Future Employability   102
                         The Net Effect of Youth Labor
                         Force Status   108
                         Notes   116
                         Appendix   117

Chapter Seven   A Reassessment of Youth
                     Unemployment   125
                         Arvil V. Adams and
                         Garth L. Mangum

                         An Overview   126
                         Lessons for Youth Employment Policy .   130
                             General Labor Market Policies   130
                             Youth Labor Market Policies   132
                                 Job Creation   132
                                 Education and Training   136
                                 Market Intervention   139
                         Additional Research Needs   141
                         A Sense of Priority   142

Bibliography   143

TABLES

2-1   Occupational and Industrial Distribution of Employed Persons, 16 to 19 Years of Age, 1950 and 1976   27

3-1   Employment Status of the Civilian Noninstitutional Population 16 to 24 Years Old, by Race: 1976   37

3-2   Labor Force Status of the Civilian Noninstitutional Population 16 to 24 Years of Age, by School Enrollment, Sex, and Age, October 1975   39

3-3   Percent of Population 16 to 24 Years of Age with Civilian Work Experience During the Year, by Sex and Age.   40

3-4   Nonagricultural Workers on Full-Time or Voluntary Part-Time Schedules, by Sex and Age   40

3-5   Long Term Unemployment Compared with Total Unemployment by Sex and Age   41

3-6   Unemployed Job Seekers by Job Search Method Used, by Sex and Age   43

3-7   Employment Status of Male Vietnam Era Veterans and Nonveterans 20 to 24 Years Old, by Race   44

3-8   Employment Status of the Civilian Noninstitutionalized Population 16 to 19 Years of Age in Metropolitan and Nonmetropolitan Areas, 1976.   46

3-9   Unemployment Rates for the Civilian Noninstitutionalized Population 16 to 19 Years Years of Age in Poverty and Nonpoverty Areas, by Race, 1976.   47

4-1   Employment by Occupation Group, 1970 and
Projected 1985 Requirements.................... 54

4-2   Occupational Distribution of Employment for
Youth 16-19 by Sex and Race, 1970.............. 57

4-3   Occupational Distribution of Employment for
Youth 20-24 by Sex and Race, 1970.............. 59

4-4   1985 Employment Projections for Youths, 16 to 24
Years of Age, by Occupation, Based
Upon the 1970 Youth Occupational Distribution
by Sex and Race.............................. 60

4-5   Youth Unemployment Projections for 1985 Based
Upon the 1970 Youth Occupational
Distribution by Age, Sex, and Race.............. 61

5-1   Percent of Youth Employed Part Time, by Sex,
Age, Race, Survey Year, and Age of Cohort 70

5-2   Last High School and Entry-Level Employment
of Males by Industry and Occupation 72

5-3   Last High School and Entry-Level Employment
of Females by Industry and Occupation 74

5-4   Labor Market Experience of 16- to 19-Year Olds
by Race, Sex, and School Enrollment Status 77

5-5   The Likelihood of Labor Force Participation and
Unemployment for 16-19 Year Old
Males and Females 82

5-6   Determinants of Teenage Labor Market
Experience by Race for Males 86

5-7   Determinants of Teenage Labor Market
Experience by Race for Females 88

6-1   Labor Force Status in Final Survey Year by Earlier
School Enrollment and Labor Force Status 104

6-2   Mean Earnings by Prior Labor Force and School
Enrollment Status for Aging Cohorts of Young
Men and Young Women Who Were Out of
School in Final Survey Year 106

6-3   Correlates of Variations in Wage and Salary
Income in Final Survey Year for Out-of-School
Young Men and Young Women 110

6-4   Adjusted Mean Earnings by Prior Labor Force
and School Enrollment Status for Aging Cohorts
of Young Men and Young Women Who Were
Out of School in Final Survey Year 112

Appendix 6-1   Employment by Occupation of Current
of Last Job by Survey Year for Young
Men Who Were 16 to 19 Years of
Age in 1966 119

Appendix 6-2   Employment by Industry of Current or
Last Job by Survey Year for Young
Men Who Were 16 to 19 Years of
Age in 1966 120

Appendix 6-3   Employment by Occupation of Current
or Last Job by Survey Year for Young
Women Who Were 16 to 19 Years of
Age in 1968 121

Appendix 6-4   Employment by Industry of Current or
Last Job by Survey Year for Young
Women Who Were 16 to 19 Years of
Age in 1968 122

Appendix 6-5   Labor Market Experience for Aging
Cohort of Males Who Were 16-19
in 1966 by Survey Year, Age, and Race ... 123

Appendix 6-6   Labor Market Experience for Aging
Cohort of Females Who Were 16-19
in 1968, by Survey Year, Age, and Race... 124

FIGURES

2-1   Relative Population Increase of Black and
All Teenagers 21

2-2   Ratio of Youth to Adult Unemployment
Rates, 1960-1976 23

2-3   Teenage Unemployment Rates by Race 25

2-4   Teenage Unemployment Rates During
the Vietnam Years 29

4-1   Projected Employment Growth of
Occupations Through the Mid-1980s 55

5-1   Civilian Labor Force Participation, School
Enrollment, and Unemployment Rates for Aging
Cohort of Males Who Were 16-19 Years of Age
in 1966 69

5-2   Civilian Labor Force Participation, School
Enrollment, and Unemployment Rates for Aging
Cohort of Females Who Were 16-19 Years
of Age in 1968 69

6-1   Percentage Distribution of Employment by
Occupation for Aging Cohorts of
Males and Females 96

6-2   Percentage Distribution of Employment by
Industry for Aging Cohorts of Males
and Females 97

6-3   Hourly Rate of Pay, Weeks Worked, and Annual
Earnings for Aging Cohorts of Young Men
and Women 16-19 Years of Age in Initial
Survey Years 101

xvii

THE
LINGERING CRISIS
OF YOUTH
UNEMPLOYMENT

THE NATURE
OF YOUTH UNEMPLOYMENT

By
Arvil V. Adams, Garth L. Mangum, and Stephen F. Seninger

The youth labor market experience typically includes some period of unemployment. In 1976 this was true for an average of 15 percent of our nation's youth 16 to 24 years of age. For those in their teens, the average rate was even higher—20 percent. For young blacks the statement seems particularly relevant. The unemployment rate among black teenagers in 1976 rose to 37 percent in comparison with that of white teenagers, 17 percent. When location is added, the rate for black teenagers in metropolitan poverty areas increases to 43 percent.

Startling as these statistics may be, they fail to reveal the true dimensions of the problem. Whereas nearly 3.4 million youths 16 to 24 years of age were unemployed, on the average, during 1976, the actual number experiencing some unemployment during the year is estimated to be twice this number. One-half of all unemployment in recent years has been accounted for by the crucial nine years from 16 to 24. This, of course, does not include those youths who would be looking for work if they thought it were available.

But one can also minimize the evidence of youth unemployment and its economic significance. Of the average 7.3 million unemployed nationally in 1976, there were 1.7 million teenagers; another 1.7 million were in their early twenties. Among black teenagers, the average number unemployed was 345 thousand. More to the point, the economic importance of these statistics in terms of personal hardships is qualified by the fact that many youths continue to live at home and attend school, seeking only part-time work. Nearly a third of all unemployed youths 16 to 24 years of age are enrolled in school. Among teenagers, the proportion approaches 50 percent, with 16 and 17 year olds reaching 90 percent.

Whether one considers these statistics significant or not, one fact is clear: as the unemployment rate for the youth of America has mounted, their dilemma has moved to the forefront of public concern in the 1970s. Each new monthly estimate of unemployment stirs demands for action. Individual blacks and black organizations have pressured Congress to halve the soaring rate of black teenage and youth unemployment. The congressional response has been to enact legislation such as the 1977 Youth Employment and Demonstration Projects Act, with its appropriation of $1 billion to be spent in 1978.

Because youth unemployment has resisted our best efforts thus far, this study seeks answers to the following questions:

1. What are the dimensions of youth unemployment and its underlying causes, its personal and social consequences?

2. Is youth unemployment merely a by-product of high adult unemployment?

3. Is the problem merely a phase through which everyone passes in the career development process, with no one suffering long term adverse effects?

4. Indeed, is the priority given to measures aimed at reducing youth unemployment warranted?

The study responds by seeking to determine the priorities that should be attached to the problem of youth unemployment. And if priorities are to be attached, to suggest which policies should be pursued. It begins in Chapter Two with a review of the trends in youth unemployment following World War II and continues in Chapter Three with a look at youth unemployment in the 1970s. Attention is focused on the social and economic forces that contribute to the youth employment problem and factors that distinguish the problem from that of adults. Combining employment and labor force projections, Chapter Four speculates on the likely pattern of youth unemployment in the 1980s.

Given this basic description of the problem and its structural dimensions, in Chapter Five the study begins searching for the underlying causes. The transition from school to work is examined, using longitudinal data for young men and women. The National Longitudinal Surveys first collected data on young men in 1966 and young women in 1968. The early labor market experience of each group is explored and correlated with characteristics of home, community, and school. In Chapter Six, the two panels of youths are followed through seven years, and the relation of early labor experience to subsequent experience is examined.

In brief, the study's results show the declining importance of youth unemployment as a policy issue for whites—but not for blacks—in the 1980s. Demographic patterns will make the problem increasingly one of blacks. Tight labor markets will reduce the problem but will not solve it. Perhaps the most important finding, as a guide to policy priorities, comes from the longitudinal analysis. Youth unemployment appears to be more than just a passing phase without consequence, as adverse early labor market experiences among out-of-school youth, controlling for education and other background characteristics, are found to be correlated with adverse subsequent experiences. In contrast to many earlier studies in the 1960s, this study finds positive effects for education and training among young blacks and whites.

As an introduction, the remainder of this chapter is devoted to a review of the underlying causes identified as contributing to the youth unemployment problem and the literature pertaining

3

thereto. Factors such as the postwar baby boom, the competitive disadvantage of youth against adult workers, and the cyclical sensitivity of youth unemployment and labor force participation are common themes which appear in most discussions of the youth unemployment dilemma. Other issues such as minimum wages, the job search process, and the problematic nature of the transition from school to work are also characteristic themes of the literature.

Expanding Youth Population

Many young people may be unemployed because there are so many of them. The postwar baby boom, continuing through the late 1950s and trending downward in the '60s, swelled the number of inexperienced new entrants to the labor market that the 1960s and '70s had to absorb. This influx—other factors being constant—would lead to downward pressure on youth wages. Forced to compete with adults, a youth wage differential would lead to the substitution of youths for adults, thereby absorbing a larger portion of the new entrants.

Some evidence exists to support the wage differential hypothesis. With somewhat mixed results, indirect evidence is provided by Stephenson, where a negative relationship between length of unemployment and the reservation wage is identified.[1] His analysis shows the reservation wage (especially for black youths) declining with the duration of unemployment. This decline, along with other factors such as attitude toward risk and willingness to accept jobs of short duration, increases the probability of finding employment. Gallaway's analysis of time series data also identifies a substitution effect for nonwhite teenagers.[2] He estimates a positive shift in demand for nonwhite teens created by an increase in their supply, relative to nonteenage male workers, and the resulting downward pressure on youth wages. The proposition of youth substitution for older workers is modeled by Kalachek.[3]

4

Growth of Aggregate Demand

Along with the possibility of downward wage flexibility, the labor market's ability to absorb the influx of youth would depend partially upon job creation and economic growth, particularly in those occupations and industrial sectors of the economy where the young are clustered. In this respect, the period of substantial economic growth during the 1960s, together with the expansion of military manpower in Vietman, acted in part to absorb the expanding youth labor force of that period. Similarly, the downturn of the economy in the 1970s, marked by the deepest recession in 40 years and following on the cutback in Vietnam, doubtless contributed to soaring youth unemployment of this period.

The responsiveness of youth unemployment to aggregate demand is a major theme of the literature. The increase in youth employment during periods of high aggregate demand is explained by Thurow in terms of a queue theory.[4] As demand increases, the most preferred workers become short in supply, and youths are then chosen from the queue. Tella offers a similar explanation where tight labor markets generate shortages of primary workers, causing employers to increase training programs and upgrade marginal workers—which reduces their unemployment relative to primary workers.[5] Kalachek, moreover, points out the increased profitability of youth, as preferred workers become more expensive.[6]

As unemployment rises and employment declines, the number of teenage workers in the labor force decreases. Perry uses time series data to analyze this tradeoff between participation and unemployment rates.[7] He estimates the percentage change in participation rates, given a sustained increase of one percentage point in a weighted unemployment rate. The teenage cohort shows the greatest sensitivity, with the teenage participation rate for males decreasing by three percentage points and by slightly more than that for females, given a one percentage point increase in the weighted unemployment rate.

5

This tradeoff causes the teenage unemployment rate to understate the number of frustrated would-be employees as argued by Tella[8] and Kalachek,[9] since more teens leave the labor force than enter the ranks of the unemployed. According to Hedges, reductions in the teenage unemployment rate during recovery come slowly, with part of this response attributed to labor force entry and reentry effects.[10] Kalachek argues that the increase in teenage labor force participation as the labor market tightens is the net result of an income-substitution effect.[11] Heads of households secure employment more easily during an upturn, their income in turn discouraging teenage participation. This discouragement among teenagers is quickly offset, however, by the increasing ease with which work can be found, leading to a rise in teenage labor force participation. Korbel[12] offers some empirical evidence in support of this, while Gramlich[13] identifies a small, negative tradeoff between the work effort of secondary workers (females and teenagers) and unemployment status for the head of the household.

However, "adequate" levels of aggregate demand are not a complete solution to the youth unemployment problem in view of evidence suggesting a structural component in the unemployed youth pool. Feldstein analyzed the white teenage unemployment rate in relation to the jobless rate for males 25 years and older, and identified an initial white teenage unemployment rate of 10 percent that increased proportionately with the adult male unemployment rate.[14] A similar specification for nonwhite teenagers generated a much higher initial unemployment rate of 24 percent, which was not statistically related to the adult unemployment rate.

From these results, Feldstein concluded that nonwhite teenagers have high unemployment rates independent of labor market conditions, a conclusion similar to Gallaway's work.[15] Smith offers more encouraging results, although his overall conclusion is not optimistic.[16] He simulates a favorable macroeconomic environment until 1980, at which time the estimated teenage unemployment rate drops to 13 percent, a jobless rate that would still be indicative of a "weak" teenage labor market since the youth jobless rate would remain triple that of adults.

Labor Market Barriers to Youth

To the extent that the downward flexibility of wages is reduced by labor market impediments preventing youth wages from falling to offset lower productivity and higher costs, this may adversely affect youth employment. Union negotiation of high wages for unskilled workers who are at the bottom of the job hierarchy is one impediment, identified by Folk, that forecloses entry by teenagers.[17] Friedlander makes a similar argument within the context of unemployed ghetto teenagers.[18]

Minimum wage legislation is the most frequently cited "market impediment" to youth employment opportunities. Feldstein argues that the minimum wage prohibits youth entrance into the market by excluding not only unqualified, low productivity youth, but even those who are willing to buy training by accepting lower wages.[19] Cottereill and Wadych, on the other hand, claim empirical evidence that actual earnings increase for teens and the substitution of older for younger workers does not develop under minimum wages.[20]

Ragan analyzes teenage unemployment data between 1963 and 1972 and concludes that the teenage unemployment rate in the latter year was 3.8 percentage points higher than it would have been in the absence of a minimum wage law.[21] Disaggregation of national data showed that male youths were affected more severely than female teenagers, and 16 and 17 year olds slightly more than 18 and 19 year olds, while nonwhite teenage males suffered the most severe unemployment effects of minimum wage laws. This relationship has also been supported by Fisher, who estimates that a decrease in the minimum wage of 15 to 20 percent might decrease the teenage unemployment rate by almost 2 percentage points.[22] Fisher points out, however, that elimination

7

of the minimum wage would not be sufficient to eliminate the problem of teenage unemployment, especially for nonwhite teenagers.

Minimum wage-induced unemployment effects have also been analyzed in terms of a differential minimum wage based on age. Gramlich's analysis suggests that minimum wages are slightly low to about right for adults, but that they are too high for teenagers.[23] Although possibly leading to the substitution of youth for adults, Gramlich views a "youth differential" in minimum wages as a reasonable policy objective that would make teenage and adult unemployment rates more equitable. Such a proposal was rejected by Congress during debate on the 1977 amendments to the Fair Labor Standards Act.

Urbanization and Minority Employment

Increased mechanization of farming has reduced employment opportunities. It has affected youths especially, particularly black youths, in rural areas. The subsequent pattern of rural to urban migration may have moved many of these young people from the uncounted to the counted unemployment roles (a member of a farm family is not as likely to be counted as unemployed during periods of inactivity, nor is a hired farmworker as likely as an urban worker to seek employment during off seasons). In an urban setting, one is less likely to be engaged in a family enterprise and more likely to seek paid employment. In contrast to a rural setting where job opportunities, or the lack thereof, are generally known, one is less likely in an urban setting to know whether employment is available and more likely to search for jobs.

Aside from the enumeration issue, urbanization has had a more direct effect upon youth employment. Mangum and Seninger identify a stabilizing urban population with a growing minority youth component that is competing for jobs within deteriorating urban labor markets.[24] Many semiskilled manufacturing jobs, traditionally a major route into employment for new entrants, are

8

no longer in the central cities, thus reducing opportunities for employment. Unlike those in rural settings, where skills and work habits were formed early through work on the farm and close observation of parents at work, youngsters in urban areas have fewer alternatives of this sort available. Kalachek views the reduced urban demand for teenage labor as a major determinant of minority teenage unemployment, with the principal victims being children of the last legal immigrant group into the cities, the blacks.[25]

A study by Levitan and Taggart focuses on the job crisis for black youth and identifies both white and nonwhite urban youth as peripheral workers characterized by intermittent or part-time, low-income employment, concentrated in low-status industries and occupations.[26] The "credentials gap" is expressed as a prime reason for the continuing disparity between nonwhite and white employment patterns, since black youths are more likely to be poorly prepared for and ill-adjusted to the world of work. Levitan and Taggart point out that the substantial gains in educational attainment of black youths have not brought commensurate improvement in their labor market status. Black youths' "credentials" are not as respected as those of white youths, a labor market prejudice supported in part by qualitative differences in education and by racial discrimination.

The ramifications of racial discrimination are explored by Brimmer[27] and by Becnel[28] who argue that the age old problem of youth unemployment is rapidly becoming a problem of black youth unemployment. Gordon offers a dual labor market argument where teenagers, particularly those in minority groups, are relegated to low-paying, unstable employment opportunities in the secondary labor market.[29] It is here that teenage male workers find themselves competing for low-skill jobs with other minorities and females who, according to Freedman, have been a growing and competitive component in the teenage labor force.[30] Racial discrimination is also discussed by Staples, who relates black youth alienation from the educational process and from the labor market to extraordinarily high involvement with criminal activities.[31] Harrison expands the simple dichotomy of primary

9

and secondary labor markets to include an "irregular" sector (or the "hustle"), where teenagers engage in a variety of illicit activities, and a "welfare" sector, where individuals receive income transfer payments in return for their investment of time.[32] The environment of the urban setting, including its market for illicit activities, is examined by Adams and Nestel and found to contribute to substantially lower earnings and work experience for urban black youth vis-a-vis rural migrant youths.[33] Similar findings are offered by Weiss and Williamson.[34]

Transition From School to Work

The longer period of fluctuation between school and work in response to an upward trend in years of schooling and the structural factors influencing this transition are potentially important factors affecting youth unemployment. Folk[35] and Kalachek[36] argue that teenage entry into the labor force plus the part-time status of many youth jobs combine to create a highly unstable employment pattern for youth, particularly in comparison to adult workers who maintain relatively stable employment relationships.

Teenagers account for a disproportionate share of job searching and, according to Freedman, change jobs and move in and out of the labor force with greater frequency than any other age group.[37] Barret and Mergenston[38] attribute some of this job switching to dissatisfaction with low pay and minimal work, while Feldstein[39] identifies increased employment stability among young workers as a necessary component of any policy aimed at reducing teenage unemployment.

Other research has related teenage employment problems to a necessary maturation process in the transition from school to work. Kalachek argues that high jobless rates for teenagers partly reflect the hunt for a first job or for a new job after a period of nonparticipation in the labor force.[40] Younger teenagers are more susceptible to unemployment than older teenagers because they

10

are usually interested in vacation jobs and other less time-restricting types of employment. Freedman suggests that intermittent entrance and reentrance into the labor force increases the chances of young teenagers joining the unemployed as reentrants rather than as job losers.[41]

The passage of time clearly reduces unemployment rates as teenagers mature and gain more labor market experience. Parnes and Kohen analyzed a longitudinal sample of 2,100 young people and found movement up the occupational ladder correlated with education, work experience, and increased amounts of labor market experience.[42] The role of family background, intelligence, and education in this transitional process have been examined by Hall and Kasten[43] and Corcoran et al.[44] Johnston and Bachman provide empirical evidence highlighting the importance of family background in the transitional process.[45] The relation between family background, income, and teenage employment is examined by Bowen and Finegan who found that teenage labor force participation dropped as family income grew from less than $2,000 to $6,000 and increased thereafter until upper income levels were reached.[46] Their explanation was that parents and friends of such teenagers were better able than those parents with lower income to help them find work.

The importance of entry-level jobs for teenagers during the transitional process has been studied by Ornstein[47] and others. Anderson[48] and Burdetsky[49] argue in terms of a basic mismatch between schooling and training (prior to entry into the labor market) and actual market skill requirements. Winter also claims that adequate jobs are available, but young workers are not qualified to fill them.[50] Bobrow suggests that an inadequate information system is partly responsible for this situation.[51] Kalachek formulates the mismatch proposition in terms of technical change which is destroying unskilled, traditional teenage entry jobs.[52] He largely discounts this proposition by arguing that every ladder has a bottom rung and that there are low echelon jobs for novices. Furthermore, most teenagers do not want, or are not eligible for, "entry jobs" because they are seeking only part-year or part-time work. Kalachek goes on to suggest that teenagers are

11

not available for a career job and that youth jobs do not necessarily lead to career jobs.

Teenage unemployment is viewed by Kalachek[53] and Johnston and Bachman[54] as playing a functional role through providing a school of "hard knocks." Teenage labor force participation, along with periodic unemployment, provides experience and work habits as a foundation to lifetime work. Youth unemployment in this context may be an inexpensive school where teens learn to adjust to the realities of the job market in searching for work and in choosing careers. Kalachek and others qualify this by asking whether high turnover and unemployment rates are a necessary part of youth employment statistics or simply poor substitutes for better counseling and job orientation, a point made by Bobrow.[55]

Youth employment problems are not unique to the United States. Reubens examines youth transition problems in European countries and observes that the transition is viewed as a movement from full-time school to full-time work.[56] American teenagers working full time in the labor market appear to change jobs more frequently than teenagers in other countries. In addition, teenagers in other countries accept and remain with jobs in the secondary labor market more readily than American youth; moreover, once they leave such jobs, which frequently involve apprenticeships, they experience less unemployment than American youth. Reubens also suggests that youth employment programs abroad offer greater variety and also depend relatively less on public service employment.[57] Dean's analysis of school-leaver problems in Britain suggests that, while the likelihood of unemployment is highest among school leavers, this is an entirely natural phenomenon.[58] The residual longer term unemployment among school leavers, however, is a new and major socioeconomic problem.

The youth unemployment dilemma in this country has been a long term, persistent problem in spite of a variety of policy actions in both the public and private sectors. A more adequate understanding of this problem can only be gained from a historical examination of the postwar record, a look at contemporary patterns and future trends, and an in-depth, longitudinal analysis of those youth who have experienced unemployment.

NOTES

1. Stanley P. Stephenson, "The Economics of Youth Job Search Behavior," *Review of Economics and Statistics,* vol. 58, no. 1 (February 1976), pp. 104-111.

2. Lowell E. Gallaway, "Unemployment Levels Among Non-White Teenagers," *Journal of Business,* vol. 42, no. 3 (July 1969), pp. 265-276.

3. Edward Kalachek, *The Youth Labor Market,* Policy Papers in Human Resources and Industrial Relations No. 12 (Ann Arbor, Mich.: Institute of Labor and Industrial Relations, University of Michigan-Wayne State University, 1969).

4. Lester Thurow, *Poverty and Discrimination* (Washington, D.C.: The Brookings Institution, 1969).

5. Alfred Tella, "Hidden Unemployment 1953-62—A Quantitative Analysis by Age and Sex: Comments," *American Economic Review,* vol. 55, no. 5 (December 1966), pp. 1235-1240.

6. Kalachek, *Youth Labor Market.*

7. George L. Perry, "Potential Output and Productivity," *Brookings Papers on Economic Activity,* 1 (1977), pp. 11-60.

8. Alfred Tella, "Labor Sensitivity to Employment by Age, Sex," *Industrial Relations* (February 1965), pp. 69-83.

9. Kalachek, *Youth Labor Market.*

10. Janice Hedges, "Youth Unemployment in the 1974-75 Recession," *Monthly Labor Review,* vol. 99 (January 1976), pp. 49-56.

11. Kalachek, *Youth Labor Market.*

12. John Korbel, "Labor Force Entry and Attachment of Young People," *Journal of American Statistical Association,* vol. 16 (March 1966), pp. 117-129.

13. Edward M. Gramlich, "The Distributional Effects of Higher Unemployment," *Brookings Papers on Economic Activity,* 2 (1974), pp. 293-336.

14. Martin S. Feldstein, "Lowering the Permanent Rate of Unemployment: A Study," Joint Economic Committee Printing, 93rd Congress, 1st Session, September 18, 1973 (Washington, D.C.: U.S. Government Printing Office, 1973).

15. Gallaway, "Unemployment Levels Among Non-White Teenagers."

16. Ralph Smith, "The Teenage Unemployment Problem—How Much will Macro Policies Matter?" in Congressional Budget Office, *The Teenage Unemployment Problem: What Are the Options* (Washington, D.C.: U.S. Government Printing Office, 1976).

17. Hugh Folk, "The Problem of Youth Unemployment," in *The Transition from School to Work* (Princeton, N.J.: Princeton University Press, 1968).

18. Stanley L. Friedlander, *Unemployment in the Urban Core: An Analysis of Thirty Cities with Policy Recommendations* (New York: Praeger Publishers, Inc., 1972).

19. Martin Feldstein, "The Economics of the New Unemployment," *The Public Interest,* no. 33 (Fall 1973), pp. 3-42.

20. Phillip Cottereill and Walter Wadych, "Teenagers and the Minimum Wage in Retail Trade," *Journal of Human Resources,* vol. XI, no. 1 (Winter 1976), pp. 69-85.

21. James F. Ragan, "Minimum Wages and the Youth Labor Market," *Review of Economics and Statistics,* vol. LIX, no. 2 (May 1977), pp. 129-136.

22. Alan Fisher, "The Problem of Teenage Unemployment," Ph.D. dissertation, (Berkeley, Calif.: University of California, August 1973).

23. Edward M. Gramlich, "Impact of Minimum Wages on Other Wages, Employment, and Family Incomes," *Brookings Papers on Economic Activity,* 2 (1976), pp. 409-461.

24. Garth L. Mangum and Stephen F. Seninger, *Coming of Age in the Ghetto: The Dilemma of Ghetto Youth Unemployment* (Baltimore, Md.: Johns Hopkins University Press, 1978).

25. Kalachek, *Youth Labor Market.*

26. Sar Levitan and Robert Taggart, "Background Paper on the Job Crisis for Black Youth," in Twentieth Century Fund Task Force on Employment Problems of Black Youth, *The Job Crisis for Black Youth* (New York: Praeger Publishers, Inc., 1971).

27. Andrew Brimmer, *The Economic Position of Black Americans: 1976,* Special Report No. 9, National Commission for Manpower Policy (Washington, D.C.: U.S. Government Printing Office, 1976).

28. Barbara Becnel, "Profiling the Black Worker, 1976," *AFL-CIO American Federationist* (July 1976), pp. 11-20.

29. David M. Gordon, *Theories of Poverty and Underemployment* (Lexington, Mass.: D.C. Heath, 1972).

30. Marcia Freedman, "Appendix: An Outline of the Issues and Policy Perspectives," in *From School to Work: Improving the Transition,* National Commission on Manpower Policy (Washington, D.C.: U.S. Government Printing Office, 1976).

31. Robert Staples, "To Be Young, Black, and Oppressed," *Black Scholar,* vol. 7, no. 10 (July 1975), pp. 39-47.

32. Bennett Harrison, "Ghetto Economic Development," *Journal of Economic Literature,* vol. XII, no. 1 (March 1974), pp. 1-37.

33. Arvil V. Adams and Gilbert Nestel, "Interregional Migration, Education, and Poverty in the Urban Ghetto: Another Look at Black-White Earnings Differentials," *Review of Economics and Statistics,* vol. LVIII, no. 2 (May 1976), pp. 156-166.

34. Leonard Weiss and J.G. Williamson, "Black Education, Earnings, and Interregional Migration: Some New Evidence," *American Economic Review,* vol. 62, no. 3 (June 1972), pp. 372-383.

35. Folk, "Problem of Youth Unemployment."

36. Kalachek, *Youth Labor Market.*

37. Marcia Freedman, "The Youth Labor Market," in *From School to Work: Improving the Transition,* National Commission on Manpower Policy (Washington, D.C.: U.S. Government Printing Office, 1975).

38. Nancy S. Barret and Richard D. Mergenston, "Why Do Blacks and Women Have High Unemployment Rates," *Journal of Human Resources,* vol. IX, no. 4 (Fall 1974), pp. 452-455.

39. Feldstein, "Economics of the New Unemployment."

40. Kalachek, *Youth Labor Market.*

41. Freedman, "Youth Labor Market."

42. Herbert S. Parnes and Andrew Kohen, "Labor Market Experience of Noncollege Youth: A Longitudinal Analysis," in *From School to Work: Improving the Transition,* National Commission for Manpower Policy (Washington, D.C.: U.S. Government Printing Office, 1975).

43. Robert E. Hall and Richard A. Kasten, "Occupational Mobility and the Distribution of Occupational Success Among Young Men," *American Economic Review,* vol. 66, no. 2 (May 1976), pp. 309-315.

44. Mary Corcoran, Christopher Jencks, and Michael Olneck, "The Effects of Family Background on Earnings," *American Economic Review,* vol. 66, no. 2 (May 1976), pp. 430-435.

45. Jerome Johnston and Jerold Bachman, *The Transition from High School to Work: The Work Attitudes and Early Occupational Experience of Young Men* (Ann Arbor, Mich.: The University of Michigan, 1973).

46. William G. Bowen and T. Aldrich Finegan, *The Economics of Labor Force Participation* (Princeton, N.J.: Princeton University Press, 1969).

16

47. Michael D. Ornstein, *Entry Into the American Labor Force* (Toronto: York University Press, 1976).

48. Bernard Anderson, "Youth Unemployment Problems in the Inner City," in Congressional Budget Office, *The Teenage Unemployment Problem: What Are the Options* (Washington, D.C.: U.S. Government Printing Office, 1976).

49. Ben Burdetsky, "Troubled Transition: From School to Work," *Worklife* (November 1976).

50. Elmer Winter, "The Businessman's Role in Closing the Gap Between Education and the Job," in *The Transition from School to Work* (Princeton, N.J.: Princeton University Press, 1968).

51. Sue Bobrow, *Reasonable Expectations: Limits on the Promise of Community Councils* (Santa Monica, Calif.: The Rand Corporation, 1976).

52. Kalachek, *Youth Labor Market.*

53. Kalachek, *Youth Labor Market.*

54. Johnston and Bachman, *Transition from High School to Work.*

55. Bobrow, *Reasonable Expectations.*

56. Beatrice Reubens, "Foreign and American Experience with the Youth Transition," in *From School to Work: Improving the Transition,* National Commission on Manpower Policy (Washington, D.C.: U.S. Government Printing Office, 1976).

57. Beatrice Reubens, "Foreign Experiences," in Congressional Budget Office, *The Teenage Unemployment Problem: What Are the Options* (Washington, D.C.: U.S. Government Printing Office, 1976).

58. A.J.H. Dean, "Unemployment Among School Leavers: An Analysis of the Problem," *National Institute Economic Review* (November 1976), pp. 63-68.

17

Postwar Trends in Youth Unemployment

By
Stephen F. Seninger

In providing an historical perspective to the youth unemployment problem, this chapter highlights the various dimensions of the problem and reviews the responses of public policy. Youth unemployment emerges as a complex socioeconomic phenomenon, deeply rooted on the supply side of the labor market in structural shifts of the population and in differences by race. On the demand side, these interact with postwar trends in occupation, industry, and economic activity.

The Postwar Baby Boom

The postwar baby boom was a major underlying force leading to the labor market problems of teenagers throughout the 1960s and 1970s. New births reached an intermediate peak in 1947, with 3.8 million live births a year, continuing to a second peak spanning four years from 1958 to 1962 of slightly under 4.5 million births a year. The first of these peaks was due to a significant increase in the number of first-born children and the second to an increasing number of second- and third-born.

A direct consequence of the population explosion was an increase in the number of teenagers during the early 1960s. This pattern continued through the mid-1970s before turning downward. The last of the baby boom population will pass through their teenage years in 1981. As shown in Figure 2-1, the teenage population will decline rapidly thereafter in relative terms, but not for blacks. Reflecting the fact that postwar birthrates for blacks peaked later and are declining more slowly than those for whites, the black teenage population will continue its present rapid growth at least through 1990. The teenage population, as such, will become increasingly black.

Population trends have created enormous pressures on the supply side of the youth labor market, pressures that have already begun to ease and will continue to dwindle rapidly after 1981. One manifestation of these pressures has been the continued and persistently high unemployment rates for teenagers throughout the 1960s to the present. The jobless rate for teenagers increased from a comparatively low 9.6 percent in 1947 to 16 percent in 1974, a rate which later increased to 20 percent during the 1974-75 recession. Over this period teenagers as a percentage of the labor force increased from 7.5 to 10. The teenage share of total unemployment grew from 18 to 22 percent.

Another measure of the influence of population trends upon youth unemployment is the changing structural relation of youth and adult unemployment rates. Youths have traditionally experienced a comparative employment disadvantage to older workers in the labor market, a disadvantage which shows up in consistently higher unemployment rates for youth vis-a-vis adults. Expansion of the youth population in the 1960s, along with relatively stable labor force participation rates, coincided with a perceptible upward shift in the youth-adult unemployment ratio.

The ratio of youth to adult unemployment remained fairly stable throughout the 1950s and into the early 1960s. Due to the

20

Figure 2-1. Relative Population Increase of Black and All Teenagers, 1970-1990

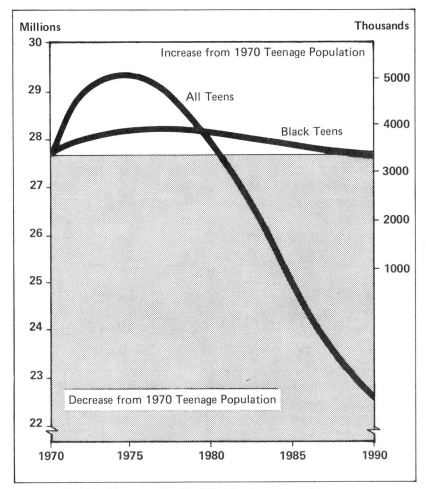

Source: Garth L. Mangum, *Employability, Employment, and Income.*

positive effects of aging upon unemployment, teenage-adult unemployment ratios were consistently higher than those for young adults 20 to 24 years of age. Beginning in 1963, however, with the entry of the baby boom population, the teenage-adult unemployment ratio rose from its previous level of approximately 3.2:1 to a record high in 1969 of 5.5:1 before returning in 1976 to its historical base (Figure 2-2). A similar, although less distinct, pattern can be observed for young adults beginning later in 1967.

The period from 1963 to 1969 was a period marked by sustained economic growth and declining unemployment. Therefore, part of the increase of the youth-adult unemployment ratio may be attributed to the response of adult unemployment to expanding employment opportunities. But the influx of youth doubtless dampened the youth labor market's ability to keep pace. The result, in sharp contrast with the earlier postwar period, was a rising ratio of teenage to adult unemployment. By 1976 the influx of teenagers had passed its peak. With the weakening of the economy, higher adult unemployment through the 1970s returned the teenage-adult unemployment ratio to its historical level.

Several conclusions can be drawn from this experience. First, the postwar baby boom was a major force underlying youth unemployment in the 1960s and 1970s. The effect of this force, however, has already begun to dissipate and will largely disappear in the 1980s. Black youth, whose population growth will continue through the 1980s at basically the same level as that in the 1970s (in contrast to whites) will become a more visible element of the youth unemployment problem. Second, the high youth unemployment rates of the mid-seventies can be attributed more to the higher general levels of unemployment than to the postwar baby boom. The return of the youth-adult unemployment ratio to its historical level reinforces this point.

Figure 2-2. Ratio of Youth to Adult Unemployment Rates, 1960-1976[a]

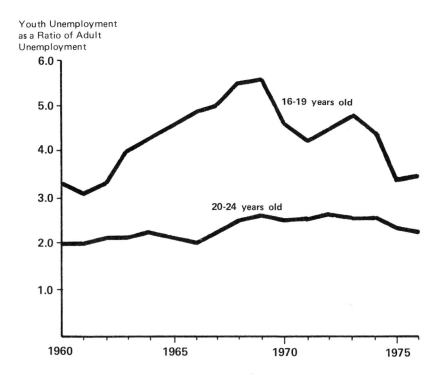

Youth Unemployment
as a Ratio of Adult
Unemployment

16-19 years old

20-24 years old

Source: 1977 Employment and Training Report of the President.

[a]Adult unemployment rates were computed for those 25 years of age and over.

Black Compared with White Youth Unemployment

To conclude that the postwar baby boom's impact upon youth unemployment will diminish in the early 1980s is not to conclude that youth unemployment itself will dissipate, only that it will become relatively less severe. The problem that remains, given teenage unemployment rates three times greater than those of adults, will become increasingly a black youth unemployment problem. Black and other nonwhite youths are expected to represent 14.6 percent of the teenage labor force in 1980, increasing to 15.2 percent in 1985, as compared with 11.1 percent in 1970. The significance of this can be seen in a comparison of unemployment rates for black and white youths.

Blacks and other minority teenagers have consistently experienced higher unemployment rates in contrast to their white counterpart. The disparity of the two jobless rates was relatively small in the mid-1950s, but increased significantly thereafter, leading to a widening gap in the unemployment of minority and white youths (Figure 2-3). In 1954 the ratio of nonwhite to white teenage unemployment was 1.3:1. This ratio increased throughout the early 1960s, reaching a value of 2.3:1 in 1966. By 1976 the ratio reached 2.2:1, with nonwhite and white teenage unemployment rates of 37 and 17 percent, respectively.

The mass migration of southern blacks to northern cities in the postwar period exacerbated the youth employment problem. Black youth became clustered in central cities, areas marked by retarded employment growth. Low to negative employment growth within key industrial and occupational categories that traditionally had been heavy employers of teenagers led to central city jobless rates considerably above the teenage unemployment rates in suburban and nonmetropolitan areas. Indeed, teenage unemployment among black youths in central cities reached 43 percent in 1976.

Figure 2-3. Teenage Unemployment Rates by Race

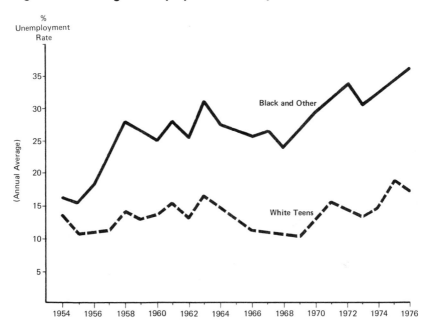

Source: 1977 Employment and Training Report of the President.

Occupation and Industry Trends

Teenage employment patterns by occupation and industry are important characteristics of the youth labor market experience. A large proportion of teenagers combines work with school, forcing them to find part-time jobs usually characterized by high turnover. The part-time nature of many teenage jobs leads to employment within certain industries that are more amenable to part-time employment arrangements. These industries are characterized by low-skill employment, high turnover, and low wages.

Postwar trends in occupational distributions show the movement of teenagers from farm to service employment and continued concentration in certain blue-collar categories and in clerical employment. These occupations currently account for nearly three-fourths of teenage employment, with service workers alone accounting for nearly 30 percent. One out of three employed teenagers remains in blue-collar occupations; when service employment is added to this figure, it becomes two out of three. Both categories are subject to above average unemployment. In terms of their industrial affiliation, teenagers are overwhelmingly concentrated in wholesale and retail trade. Four out of ten teenage jobs are found in this sector, jobs also characterized by above average unemployment.

Changes in Economic Activity

With the rapid expansion of the teenage population in the mid-1960s, teenage unemployment became a major issue. The full effect of this expansion, however, was partially offset by two events: the Kennedy tax cut of 1964 and the escalation of the Vietnam War. Both were important to what otherwise would have been a much more serious teenage unemployment problem. The Vietnam War had a major impact on the nation's labor force in the mid-1960s, an impact which is usually dated from 1965 to the end of the decade. The Vietnam conflict directly increased defense

26

Table 2-1. Occupational and Industrial Distribution of Employed Persons, 16 to 19 Years of Age, 1950 and 1976

Occupational	1950	1976
Total, all occupations	100.0	100.0
Professional and technical	3.0	2.3
Managerial	1.0	1.1
Sales	11.0	8.7
Clerical	21.0	19.2
Craft	4.0	5.7
Operatives	19.0	14.0
Laborers, non-farm	8.6	14.0
Laborers, farm	18.9	4.6
Service	13.0	29.6

Industrial	1950	1976
Total	100.0	100.0
Agriculture	20.5	4.5
Mining	0.7	0.3
Construction	3.5	3.9
Manufacturing	21.3	13.5
Transportation and public utilities	4.7	1.8
Wholesale and retail trade	26.0	43.4
Finance, insurance and real estate	4.3	3.4
Services	17.0	20.8
Government	1.4	8.4

Sources: U.S. Department of Labor and U.S. Department of Commerce.

employment and indirectly generated more jobs in defense-related industries. These employment effects, along with an increase in the size of the Armed Forces, led to lower total unemployment rates. When joined with the effects of the Kennedy tax cut, this produced a decline in the nation's unemployment rate for those 16 years of age and over from 5.2 percent in 1964 to 3.5 percent in 1969.

Reductions in the youth unemployment rate during this period were even more pronounced. Teenage unemployment rates declined from 16.2 percent in 1964 to approximately 12 percent in 1969. Unemployment among black and white teenagers during this period followed the same course, with white teenage unemployment dropping by four percentage points, while that for minority youths declined by slightly more than three percentage points.

The dampening effect of Vietnam on teenage unemployment was stronger for young males 18 to 19 years of age who were more directly affected by increased military manpower requirements. Among white males in this age group, for example, unemployment decreased by nearly six percentage points, from 13.4 percent in 1964 to 7.9 percent in 1969. Minority males in this age group experienced a somewhat smaller decrease, from a jobless rate of 23 percent in 1964 to 19 percent in 1969. The decrease in unemployment for those 16 to 17 years of age was more moderate, declining from 17.8 to 14.5 percent.

The cushioning effect of an expansionary economy and Vietnam on a large teenage labor force was apparent in the higher youth unemployment rates which characterized the turn of the decade. Withdrawal from Vietnam, along with an immediate postwar recession, contributed to an upward shift in teenage unemployment. This shift was particularly pronounced for the male teen jobless rate which increased by 3.6 percentage points in 1970, an unfavorable increase when compared to a lower 2.3 percentage point increase for female teenagers. This upward shift and the continued high unemployment rate for youths during the 1970s were inextricably tied to the downturn of the nation's economic activity following withdrawal from Vietnam.

Figure 2-4. Teenage Unemployment Rates During the Vietnam Years

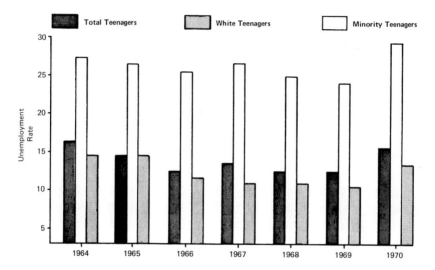

Source: 1977 Employment and Training Report of the President.

Two patterns emerge from the experience of the 1969-70 postwar recession. First, the youth unemployment rate moved to its highest level since the baby boom entry effect of 1963. Teenage unemployment remained above 16 percent in 1971 and 1972, with a moderate drop below 15 percent in 1973. Second, this new unemployment plateau for youths set the stage for an even higher teenage unemployment rate in the ensuing recession of 1974-75.

In the second post-Vietnam recession (1974-75), teenage unemployment rates increased, along with jobless rates for young adults and adult workers. The teenage unemployment rate increased from a low of 14.3 percent in the last quarter of 1973 to a high of 20 percent during the first half of 1975. Most important, these unemployment increases occurred in the presence of a teenage population increase of only 10 percent between 1970 and 1975, or roughly half that of a similar period in the 1960s.

As such, the 1974-75 recession represents the most recent and the highest cyclical peak in a secular, upward trend of youth jobless rates over the postwar period. The 20 percent unemployment rate for teenagers in 1975 represents an unprecedentedly high jobless rate for all years starting with 1947. As suggested here, however, this increase can be attributed first to the influx of youths during the 1960s, and second to the downturn of economic activity in the 1970s. With the diminished importance of youth population expansion in the 1970s, it is the downturn of economic activity and the deeper structural problems underlying youth-adult unemployment experiences to which public policy must now be directed.

Other Postwar Trends

Other factors have contributed to postwar youth unemployment trends. Increasing labor force participation of women, from 32.7 percent in 1948 to 47.3 percent by 1976, doubtless contributed to the secular rise of youth unemployment by enlarging the competition for youth jobs. Added to this was the growing competition from undocumented workers in the 1960s. Alongside these trends was the continued heavy shift of population from rural-farm to urban locations with the consequent loss of farm work opportunity for many young people. Offsetting these trends, in part, was the declining labor force participation of men, especially of blacks and the elderly. The net result, however, has been a secular increase of youth unemployment over the postwar period.

Policy Response

Youth unemployment first emerged as a high priority public policy concern in 1963 with the first of the baby boom cohort reaching 16 years of age. Unemployment of married men, which had been at 4.6 percent in 1961, had declined to 3.4 percent by 1963, yet overall unemployment had actually risen from 5.5 percent in 1962 to 5.7 percent in 1963. The essential reason was that teenage unemployment, which had been 14.7 percent in 1962, had risen to 17.2 percent by 1963. Conant had coined the phrase "social dynamite" in regard to central city youth unemployment rates, and the stage was set for policy responses.

Policymakers looked back to the 1930s for that response. The Civilian Conservation Corps had enrolled young men in a semimilitary atmosphere, housed them in barracks, and employed them in the forests and similar areas. The National Youth Administration had given in-school youths part-time janitorial employment and offered other minor public work activities to those out of school. The resurrection of such programs was proposed in a Youth Employment Act of 1963, including a Youth Conservation Corps and a Hometown Youth Corps.

The bill easily passed the Senate but was bottled up in a conservative-dominated House Rules Committee which had a manifest distaste for social programs. The Manpower Development and Training Act (MDTA) of the previous year had been limited by law to no more than five percent youths. Now that ceiling was lifted to 25 percent. The Vocational Education Act of 1963 rounded out the youth oriented legislation of the year. It was a long term reform, using the new concern for youth unemployment to shift the emphasis of vocational education from those occupations needing skilled workers to the population groups needing employment.

Then came 1964, the antipoverty year. War was declared on poverty before consideration was given to the choice of weapons. Labor Department representatives on the task force designing the Economic Opportunity Act (EOA) advocated the provisions of the previous year's Youth Employment Act. The Hometown Youth Corps became the Neighborhood Youth Corps and the Youth Conservation Corps became the Conservation Centers of the Job Corps. The Defense Department, faced with the painful necessity of closing idle military bases, proposed that they be used as residential vocational schools—the Job Corps Urban Centers.

Thus, the manpower programs of the 1960s carried a heavy youth emphasis, with over one-third of the MDTA enrollees being less than 22 years of age and almost all of the enrollments in the remaining programs named falling into that age category. From its beginning, until replaced by the Comprehensive Employment and Training Act (CETA) in 1974, MDTA enrolled 575,500 youths 21 and under in classroom skill training and 170,200 in on-the-job training. The Neighborhood Youth Corps provided work experience in rudimentary tasks to 1.3 million in-school and 842,000 out-of-school youths, with 3.6 million enrolled during summers. A quarter of a million youths learned job skills, basic education, and "group living" in the Job Corps. Over the same period, annual vocational education enrollments rose from 4 million to 12 million.

The results of these activities are not entirely clear, but the millions of dollars spent on evaluation provided useful generalizations. MDTA studies, in general, indicated a highly favorable ratio of benefits to costs, one of the largest studies showing an average annual earnings gain of $2,000 for the 19 to 21 year old enrollees.[1] The Neighborhood Youth Corps supplied

32

income and useful activities to poor youths during a difficult and critical time of their lives, but probably had little long term influence on their employability. Those observers who called it an "aging vat" were not being critical.[2] The Job Corps began as the most criticized of programs and later became one of the most popular.[3] After initial start-up problems, its administrators did learn how to recruit youth from the most disadvantaged backgrounds, acculturate them, give them job skills, and achieve positive placements in schools, the military, and jobs for a considerable proportion of them. All of that experience provided a base for the decentralized approaches of CETA.

CETA changed the basic approach from categorical, federally designed programs to locally planned efforts to meet the highest priority needs as perceived by state, county, or city governments. Available was a locally determined combination of classroom and on-the-job skill training, basic education, work experience, and public service employment. That youth unemployment was generally perceived as high priority is indicated by the fact that 57 percent of the 1976 enrollees in the CETA Title I programs were under 21 years of age. Title I funding can be used for any manpower purpose and no data are available on services provided by age. However, anecdotal evidence indicates that most are enrolled in work experience programs, but with substantial elements of basic education and on-the-job training included. The public service employment components under Title II and VI enrolled only 22 percent under 22 years. Of course the 820,000 in the summer program and the 43,000 in the Job Corps of 1976 were all youths.

In 1977 Congress and the administration rediscovered youth unemployment which, while it had not expanded relative to the level of adult unemployment, had persisted at above 15 percent for three years, consequent to the persisting 7 percent overall unemployment level. But in the years since the topic had been legislatively addressed in 1963 and 1964, training had fallen into general disrepute at the national level. Public job creation was now the thing, and youths were not getting a large share of it. The Youth Employment and Demonstration Projects Act (YEDPA) called for a Youth-Adult Conservation Corps, employing youths in forest settings, a Community Improvement Program employing youths in activities such as the rehabilitation of public facilities in urban areas, and a program for which state and local CETA program operators could competitively propose employment demonstration projects. In addition to the 200,000 youth jobs contemplated in the package, a doubling of the Job Corps to above 70,000 and an undefined but required linkage with educational institutions represented a reduced but continuing training and education component. A later addition was a $400 million program to subsidize private employment for youths. At the same time, the administration was opposing enlargement of federal vocational education appropriations and categorical funding for career education.

Clearly, no one knew what to do about youth unemployment, but policymakers still felt compelled to try. Perhaps more careful examination of the incidence and impacts of youth unemployment will provide insights from which policy improvements can emerge.

NOTES

1. Garth L. Mangum and John Walsh, *A Decade of Manpower Development and Training* (Salt Lake City, Utah: Olympus Publishing Company, 1973).

2. Sar A. Levitan and Garth L. Mangum, *Federal Work and Training Programs in the Sixties* (Ann Arbor, Mich.: Institute of Labor and Industrial Relations, University of Michigan, 1969).

3. Sar A. Levitan, William B. Johnston, and Robert Taggart, *The Job Corps: A Social Experiment That Works* (Baltimore, Md.: Johns Hopkins University Press, 1975).

34

A Look
at Youth Unemployment
in the Mid-1970s

By
Arvil V. Adams and Wayne Stevenson

With unemployment among the nation's youths having reached its postwar peak in the mid-1970s, it is necessary to examine in greater detail the characteristics and activities of unemployed youths during this period. Major differences between youths and adult groups can be found with regard to the role of employment in their lives, the nature of their employment and unemployment experiences, and the methods and intensity of their job search. Moreover, the incidence of unemployment is found to be unevenly distributed within the youth population.

Like most years, 1976, on which most of the comparisons in this chapter are based, was not a typical year. The economic recovery that began in 1975 had gained strength, and total civilian employment had grown by 2.7 million. Most of this growth took place in the first two quarters of 1976, after which the expansion slowed somewhat. The unemployment rate for 1976 averaged 7.7 percent, down from the 1975 level of 8.5 percent, but still well above the pre-recession level of 4.9 percent in 1973. Employment gains during the expansion failed to produce desired reductions in unemployment largely because of the rapid increase in the size of the labor force. Much of this increase can be accounted for by new entrants or reentrants to the labor force, as reflected in an all-time high labor force participation rate of 62.1 percent. These trends were also reflected in and greatly affected labor market conditions for young Americans.

Population and Labor Force Participation

Nearly nine million teenagers were employed or looking for work in 1976, along with 13.9 million young adults 20 to 24 years of age (Table 3-1). Another 1.1 million youths 18 to 24 were in the military and not included in this count. From the population of both groups, one out of two teenagers and three out of four young adults were involved in these activities. Differences can be found by race, however. For both age groups the likelihood of labor force participation was substantially higher among whites than among blacks, perhaps reflecting greater job discouragement or possibly undercounting of labor force activity among black youths. For teenagers, the difference is striking, with the labor force participation of whites (57.6 percent) exactly 20 percentage points higher than that for blacks (37.6 percent). From a different perspective, based upon population, one out of four black teenagers was employed in 1976, in contrast with one out of two whites.

American youths continued a trend in 1975 of combining labor force participation with school. This pattern holds for young women as well as for young men. Nearly 28 percent of all youths 16 to 19 years of age (4.5 million) combined these activities, as compared with 22 percent a decade earlier. More and more youths are making the transition gradually rather than leaving school to begin a job. As might be expected, the labor force participation rates of youths not enrolled in school are higher than for enrolled

36

Table 3-1. Employment Status of the Civilian Noninstitutional Population 16 to 24 Years Old, by Race: 1976 (thousands)

Age and selected labor force characteristics	Total	Black and other	White
16 to 24 years:			
Civilian noninstitutional population	35,086	5,054	30,032
Civilian labor force	22,916	2,662	20,254
Percent of population	(65.3)	(52.7)	(67.4)
Employment	19,545	1,950	17,595
Unemployment	3,371	712	2,659
Unemployment rate	(14.7)	(26.7)	(13.1)
Not in labor force	12,170	2,392	9,779
16 to 19 years:			
Civilian noninstitutional population	16,426	2,473	13,952
Civilian labor force	8,970	931	8,039
Percent of population	(54.6)	(37.6)	(57.6)
Employment	7,269	586	6,683
Unemployment	1,701	345	1,356
Unemployment rate	(19.0)	(37.1)	(16.9)
Not in labor force	7,455	1,542	5,914
20 to 24 years:			
Civilian noninstitutional population	18,660	2,581	16,080
Civilian labor force	13,946	1,731	12,215
Percent of population	(74.7)	(67.1)	(76.0)
Employment	12,276	1,364	10,912
Unemployment	1,670	367	1,303
Unemployment rate	(12.0)	(21.2)	(10.7)
Not in labor force	4,715	850	3,865

Source: U.S. Department of Labor, *1977 Employment and Training Report of the President.*

students (Table 3-2). Whereas 44 percent of those 16 to 24 years of age enrolled in school were employed or looking for work, 77.8 percent not enrolled were engaged in such activities. However, this pattern was more pronounced for young men than for young women.

Young Employed

Based upon the ratio of employment to population, an average of 43 percent of all teenagers was employed in 1975, along with 64 percent of young adults 20 to 24 years of age. However, the magnitude of flows into and out of the youth labor market and the extent of the youth employment experience are not reflected in these data. As shown in Table 3-3, the proportion of those youths with some work experience during the year is substantially higher than that for the annual average, although slightly lower for young women than for young men.

With nearly one out of three youths in the labor force enrolled in school, the type of employment sought could be expected to vary substantially from that of adults. For the most part, this employment is temporary or part time in nature. Temporary jobs during the summer are combined with part-time work during the school year. This is particularly true among employed teenagers, 16 to 17 years of age, nine out of ten of whom are enrolled in school (Table 3-4). Whereas just over 3 percent of the employed labor force is comprised of employed teenagers 16 and 17 years of age, they represent less than 0.5 percent of those employed in full-time schedules and more than 8 percent of those employed part time voluntarily.

Young Unemployed

Young job seekers averaged 3.4 million in 1976, a figure almost evenly divided between teenagers and young adults. Nonwhites are represented more heavily (21 percent) than their share of that age population (14 percent). Furthermore, the unemployment

Table 3-2. Labor Force Status of the Civilian Noninstitutional Population 16 to 24 Years of Age, by School Enrollment, Sex, and Age, October 1975 (thousands)

Enrollment status	Total	Male			Female		
		16-17	18-19	20-24	16-17	18-19	20-24
Enrolled:							
Civilian noninstitutional population	15,283	3,811	1,940	2,334	3,587	1,825	1,786
Civilian labor force	6,728	1,589	814	1,195	1,396	750	984
Percent of population	(44.0)	(41.7)	(42.0)	(51.2)	(38.9)	(41.1)	(55.0)
Employed	5,716	1,312	699	1,050	1,129	633	893
Unemployed	1,012	277	115	144	268	118	90
Unemployment rate	(15.0)	(17.4)	(14.1)	(12.1)	(19.2)	(15.7)	(9.1)
Not enrolled:							
Civilian noninstitutional population	19,417	390	1,951	6,499	525	2,308	7,744
Civilian labor force	15,105	294	1,780	6,075	250	1,545	5,161
Percent of population	(77.8)	(75.4)	(91.2)	(93.5)	(47.6)	(66.9)	(66.6)
Employed	12,851	189	1,448	5,310	155	1,251	4,498
Unemployed	2,255	105	331	766	94	293	666
Unemployment rate	(14.9)	(35.7)	(18.6)	(12.6)	(37.6)	(19.0)	(12.9)

Source: U.S. Department of Labor, 1977 Employment and Training Report of the President.

Table 3-3. Percent of Population 16 to 24 Years of Age with Civilian Work Experience During the Year, by Sex and Age (1975)

Age	Total	Male	Female
16 to 17	50.1	54.1	46.0
18 to 19	75.0	90.2	70.1
20 to 24	81.0	88.9	73.6

Source: U.S. Department of Labor, *1977 Employment and Training Report of the President.*

Table 3-4. Nonagricultural Workers on Full-Time or Voluntary Part-Time Schedules, by Sex and Age (1976)

Sex and age	Full time	Percent	Voluntary part time	Percent
Total:				
Number	64,810	100.0	10,942	100.0
Male:		64.8		30.9
Under 18 years		0.5		8.4
18 to 24		10.1		10.9
25 to 44		31.7		3.4
45 to 64		21.4		3.4
65 years and over		1.1		4.8
Female:		35.2		69.1
Under 18 years		0.3		8.6
18 to 24		7.8		14.0
25 to 44		15.7		24.9
45 to 64		10.9		17.2
65 years and over		0.6		4.4

Source: U.S. Department of Labor, *1977 Employment and Training Report of the President.*

experience differs with age. As shown in Table 3-5, the incidence of unemployment of 15 weeks or longer is highest among adults 25 years of age and over and lowest among teenagers. Teenage unemployment tends to be of shorter term, consistent with a pattern of high turnover and frequent job search.

In 1976, nearly 70 percent of all unemployed 16 to 19 year olds were new entrants or reentrants to the labor force. Roughly 40 percent had never worked before. In comparison, only 12 percent of nationwide unemployed workers of all ages had never worked before, with another 26 percent reentering the work force after some interruption. While half of all unemployed workers lost their

Table 3-5. Long-Term Unemployment Compared with Total Unemployment by Sex and Age (1976)

Sex and age	Number unemployed	Percent unemployed 15 weeks and over
Total:	7,288	32.1
Male:	3,965	35.7
16 to 17	437	14.0
18 to 19	488	23.0
20 to 24	926	33.6
25 to 44	1,312	40.3
45 to 64	707	50.2
65 years and over	95	49.5
Female:	3,323	27.8
16 to 17	350	12.6
18 to 19	423	19.4
20 to 24	743	24.4
25 to 44	1,188	30.5
45 to 64	554	41.0
65 years and over	51	54.9

Source: U.S. Department of Labor, *1977 Employment and Training Report of the President.*

last job, only 23 percent of all teenagers left their last job involuntarily.[1] Thus, much of the unemployment experienced by youth can be attributed to the job search effort associated with job turnover, interruptions in employment, and initial labor market entry.

Important differences can also be found in the methods used by youth to seek employment and in the intensity of their search in comparison to adults. Most important, perhaps, given the role of the federal-state employment service in providing assistance to youths under the Comprehensive Employment and Training Act, is the apparent reluctance of youths to use this method of job search. As shown in Table 3-6, teenagers are less likely than other job seekers to use a public employment agency in the job search and more likely to apply directly to employers. To the extent that it reflects intensity of search, the average number of methods used by teenagers indicates a less intensive search than that of other job seekers. On the other hand, this may simply measure the transitory nature of the youth labor market, where little search is required before additional employment is found.

The incidence of unemployment among youths is greater for some groups than others. As indicated in Table 3-2, the likelihood of incurring unemployment is greater for youths who are not enrolled in school than for those enrolled. This difference, however, narrows as young men and women grow older. Among youths 16 to 17 years of age, those not enrolled in school are twice as likely to experience unemployment as those enrolled. In all likelihood, many of the youths not enrolled at this age are school dropouts, having completed less than four years of high school.

School enrollment status also has a significant impact on the type of work sought. More than 50 percent of all unemployed 16 to 21 year olds enrolled in school were looking for temporary jobs, and less than 10 percent were looking for work because they had lost their last job. In contrast, nearly a third of all out-of-school youth had lost a job. Another 15 percent had quit (compared to 7.4 percent for those in school), and only 6 percent were looking for temporary work.[2]

Table 3-6. Unemployed Job Seekers by Job Search Method Used, by Sex and Age (1976)

Sex and age	Total job seekers (thousands)	Percent using method						Average number of methods used
		Public emp. agency	Private emp. agency	Employer directly	Friends or relatives	Placed or answered ads	Other	
Total all ages:	6,112	28.1	6.4	72.0	14.9	30.4	6.3	1.58
16 to 19	1,572	17.6	3.8	79.1	13.4	25.6	4.4	1.44
20 to 24	1,431	31.9	6.8	71.8	14.7	34.0	4.8	1.64
Total males:	3,212	30.5	6.5	73.1	17.4	28.3	8.2	1.64
16 to 19	847	17.4	3.1	80.1	15.6	24.2	4.4	1.46
20 to 24	760	34.2	6.2	73.7	17.6	31.4	5.8	1.69
Total females:	2,900	25.3	6.2	70.8	12.2	32.8	4.1	1.51
16 to 19	726	18.0	4.7	76.9	10.7	27.1	4.4	1.42
20 to 24	672	29.3	7.4	69.8	11.5	36.9	3.6	1.59

Source: U.S. Department of Labor, 1977 Employment and Training Report of the President.

Although the Vietnam War acted to soften the impact of the influx of youth upon youth unemployment during the 1960s, the long term effect of the war was to prolong the problem among young returning veterans. For Vietnam era veterans 20 to 24 years of age, a higher incidence of unemployment (about 50 percent higher) is found in a comparison of black and white veterans with nonveterans (Table 3-7). This difference all but disappears between older veterans and nonveterans. In 1976 there were 941,000 Vietnam veterans working or looking for work in the 20-24 age group. Over 17 percent of these, 164,000, were looking for work.

Table 3-7. Employment Status of Male Vietnam Era Veterans and Nonveterans 20 to 24 Years Old, by Race, 1976 (thousands)

Veteran status	Total	Black and other	White
Veterans:			
Civilian noninstitutional population	1,086	172	914
Civilian labor force	941	131	810
Percent of population	(86.6)	(76.2)	(88.6)
Employed	777	96	681
Unemployed	164	35	129
Unemployment rate	(17.4)	(26.7)	(15.9)
Not in labor force	145	40	105
Nonveterans:			
Civilian noninstitutional population	7,909	986	6,923
Civilian labor force	6,725	777	5,948
Percent of population	(85.0)	(78.8)	(85.9)
Employed	5,966	624	5,342
Unemployed	759	153	606
Unemployment rate	(11.3)	(19.7)	(10.2)
Not in labor force	1,185	209	976

Source: U.S. Department of Labor, *1977 Employment and Training Report of the President.*

Greater than the effects of the Vietnam War have been the effects of the economic war occurring in the nation's central cities, with low or even negative growth of employment occurring there. The effect upon unemployment, particularly among teenagers, has been devastating. Unemployment rates among teenagers in central cities in 1976 were substantially higher than among teenagers in the suburbs and nonmetropolitan areas (Table 3-8). In addition, because of the lower labor force participation rates among teenagers in central cities, hidden unemployment due to discouragement of job search and withdrawal from the labor force is prevalent.

The employment-population ratio, as such, offers another measure of the labor force utilization of teenagers in central cities and elsewhere. The results provide further evidence of the employment disadvantages faced by central city youths. Less than 39 percent of the central city teenage population were employed in 1976, compared with 44 percent in nonfarm areas, 47 percent in the suburbs, and 50 percent in farm areas.

If more evidence is needed concerning the problems of central city youths, it can be found in unemployment rates for poverty and nonpoverty areas. These rates are higher for metropolitan poverty areas than for any other comparison group (Table 3-9). They further illustrate the problems of black teenagers in the central city poverty environment. The unemployment rate for this group in 1976 reached an average of 43 percent!

Table 3-8. Employment Status of the Civilian Noninstitutionalized Population 16 to 19 Years of Age in Metropolitan and Nonmetropolitan Areas, 1976 (thousands)

Selected labor force characteristics	Metropolitan areas			Nonmetropolitan areas		
	Total	Central cities	Suburbs	Total	Farm	Nonfarm
Civilian noninstitutionalized population	11,172	4,521	6,651	5,253	600	4,653
Civilian labor force	6,128	2,285	3,843	2,842	320	2,522
Percent of population	(54.9)	(50.5)	(57.8)	(54.1)	(53.3)	(54.2)
Employed	4,906	1,751	3,155	2,363	300	2,063
Unemployed	1,222	535	687	479	20	459
Unemployment rate	(19.9)	(23.4)	(17.9)	(16.8)	(6.3)	(18.2)
Not in labor force	5,044	2,236	2,808	2,411	280	2,131

Source: U.S. Department of Labor, *1977 Employment and Training Report of the President.*

Table 3-9. Unemployment Rates for the Civilian Noninstitutionalized Population 16 to 19 Years of Age in Poverty and Nonpoverty Areas, by Race, 1976

Race	Total, United States		Metropolitan areas		Nonmetropolitan areas	
	Poverty areas	Nonpoverty areas	Poverty areas	Nonpoverty areas	Poverty areas	Nonpoverty areas
Total	24.1	17.9	33.2	18.6	18.6	16.0
Black	40.0	34.5	43.3	35.2	33.8	30.8
White	17.6	16.8	22.9	17.3	15.7	15.3

Source: U.S. Department of Labor, *1977 Employment and Training Report of the President.*

Reviewing the Evidence

Clearly, for most youths the employment and unemployment experience is different from that of adults. More than half of all teenagers working or looking for work are still in school; the type of work sought is largely part time; and while they are more frequent, the periods of unemployment are of shorter duration. The transition from school to work is gradual, with frequent interruptions in labor force participation. In this context, some youth unemployment can and should be thought of as a natural part of the process of assimilation by the world of work.

To the extent that the job search process and frequent job turnover contribute to a better understanding of the operation of labor markets, providing contacts and occupational information, some teenage unemployment might be thought of as beneficial in the long run. However, for teenagers and young adults who are out of school and providing for themselves, periods of unemployment may represent serious economic hardships.

The priority that public policy attaches to the problem will depend upon one's view and understanding of economic hardship. Some assess the economic hardship of unemployment in terms of its threat to the acquisition of adequate food, housing, and other necessities. Others view it as it relates to the distribution of income, while still others emphasize the psychological hardship to the individual and the lost output to society. Perhaps more important than any of these considerations, however, is the potential long term effect of youth unemployment upon the skills, attitudes, and aspirations of the individual. This relationship is examined in Chapter 6.

Among the lessons to be drawn from this review of youth unemployment in the mid-1970s is the need to target policies toward special youth populations upon whom the burden of unemployment falls heaviest. Chief among these are central city youth. Accounting for one out of every three unemployed teenagers, the youth unemployment problem in central cities, particularly among black teenagers, is reaching crisis proportions.

48

An emphasis of public policy upon central city youth is urgently needed.

The youth unemployment problem among black Americans in general, without regard to place of residence, is real. Two out of every ten unemployed youth 16 to 24 years of age are black. Black youth unemployment rates are more than twice those of whites. Postwar trends upward in the black-white teenage unemployment ratio and the continued expansion of the black teenage population expected through the 1980s point clearly to the need for targeting employment policies toward this population.

Added to this is the need to focus special attention upon out-of-school teenagers, black and white. The incidence of unemployment among the youngest of this group, those 16 to 17 years of age, is roughly twice that of their in-school counterpart. In addition, attention might be given to young Vietnam veterans. Whether their above average unemployment will diminish as they grow older, as it appears to have among older Vietnam veterans, remains to be seen.

NOTES

1. U.S. Department of Labor, *Groups with Historically High Incidence of Unemployment* (Washington, D.C.: Employment Standards Administration, July 1977).

2. U.S. Department of Labor, Bureau of Labor Statistics, *Students, Graduates, and Dropouts in the Labor Market, October 1975,* Special Labor Force Report 191 (Washington, D.C.: U.S. Government Printing Office, 1976). Table P.

4

A Changing Economy and Its Effect Upon Youth Unemployment in the Eighties

By
Stephen Mangum and Arvil V. Adams

The previous chapters show where we have been and where we are, but what lies ahead? The U.S. economy is changing rapidly. Total employment is expected to increase from its 1976 level of 87.5 million to 103.4 million by 1985, an increase of 18 percent. The number of white-collar workers is projected to increase by 22 percent during this period, with an equal increase expected for service workers. In contrast, the number of blue-collar workers, the second largest major occupational cluster, is expected to increase by only 17 percent. Among farm workers, a 33 percent decline is anticipated.

By 1985, white-collar workers are expected to account for nearly 52 percent of the nation's total employment, increasing from just under 50 percent in 1976. Service workers' share of total employment is expected to increase from 13.7 percent to slightly more than 14 percent, while the blue-collar share is expected to decline from just under 35 percent to less than 33 percent. Farm workers will account for less than 2 percent of total employment in 1985, dropping from 3.2 percent in 1976.

These changes in the occupational structure of the U.S. economy reflect trends set in motion earlier in the nation's history by industrialization and urbanization, trends that accelerated after World War II, but that are constantly shifting under the impacts of changing relative resource prices, technological change, consumer tastes, population shifts, institutional developments, and other factors. How are these changes likely to affect youth unemployment in the 1980s? What will happen to the jobs that young people held in the 1970s? To what extent will youth unemployment in the 1980s depend upon occupational upgrading and movement of the young into new occupations? How will black youths, 44 percent of whom were concentrated in slow growth, blue-collar occupations at the outset of the 1970s, fare against white youths, only 36 percent of whom were in such occupations?

Combining employment and labor force projections prepared by the Bureau of Labor Statistics (BLS) for 1985, this chapter examines these questions. Employment projections by occupation for those 16 years of age and over in 1985 are multiplied by the youth share of employment in each occupation in 1970, by race and sex, to estimate youth employment in 1985. This approach yields estimates of youth employment for 1985, assuming no change in the occupational distribution of youth by race and sex from that observed at the beginning of the 1970s. These estimates are then compared with youth labor force projections by race and sex for 1985, and unemployment estimates are derived.

The results are striking. Without substantial increases in the youth share of fast-growing white-collar and service employment by 1985, youth unemployment will remain a serious problem overwhelmingly concentrated among young blacks. Public policies concerned with the occupational mobility of youths will be an important response to the youth employment dilemma.

Employment and Labor Force Projections

In its employment and labor force projections, the Bureau of Labor Statistics begins with the present population, since everyone to be employed over the next 15 years must be alive now. Because labor force participation rates change relatively slowly, it is possible to predict with reasonable accuracy the size of the labor force several years into the future. Assuming an unemployment rate based on the present policy outlook, BLS then projects the total employment requirements for the target year. These requirements are distributed by occupation and industry, based on a projection of past trends adjusted by present indicators of likely change, considering technological development, changing population structure, observed shifts in consumer preferences, and similar factors.

The outlook for employment by occupation in 1985 for the labor force 16 years of age and over is shown in Table 4-1, along with actual employment in 1970. The BLS employment projection for 1985 is based upon a 4.8 percent unemployment rate. Alternatively, employment growth rates by occupation are shown in Figure 4-1. Substantial growth is expected in services, clerical, managers and administrators, and professional and technical occupations. White-collar employment will continue to increase faster than blue-collar employment, and farm work will decline in both absolute and relative terms.

The importance of this to youth employment depends upon the extent to which young people share in the employment of growth occupations. If youths are presently clustered in slow or no growth occupations and unable to penetrate those growing most rapidly, their employment will lag behind. Even if they find their way into growth occupations, there is no guarantee that they will share in the growth, given the diversity of trends within each broad occupational group. Service workers, for example, range from dishwashers, waiters, bellhops, cleaning personnel, and baggage porters to practical nurses, dental assistants, and police protection personnel. Clerical workers range from file clerks, stock clerks, and cashiers to bank tellers, bookkeepers, insurance adjusters, and clerical supervisors.

Table 4-1. Employment by Occupation Group, 1970 and Projected 1985 Requirements (thousands)

Occupation	Actual 1970		Projected 1985[a]	
	Number	Percent distribution	Number	Percent distribution
Total employment	76,554	100.0	103,400	100.0
Professional and technical workers	11,351	14.8	16,000	15.5
Managers and administrators, except farm	6,371	8.3	10,900	10.5
Sales workers	5,495	7.2	6,300	6.1
Clerical workers	13,748	18.0	20,100	19.4
Craft and kindred workers	10,609	13.9	13,800	13.3
Operatives	13,456	17.6	15,200	14.7
Nonfarm laborers	3,431	4.5	4,800	4.6
Service workers	9,772	12.7	14,600	14.1
Farmers and farmworkers	2,367	3.1	1,900	1.8

Source: 1970 Census of Population, *1977 Employment and Training Report of the President*, p. 259, Table E-9.
[a]Employment projections for 1985 are based upon a 4.8 percent unemployment rate.

Figure 4-1. Projected Employment Growth of Occupations Through the Mid-1980s

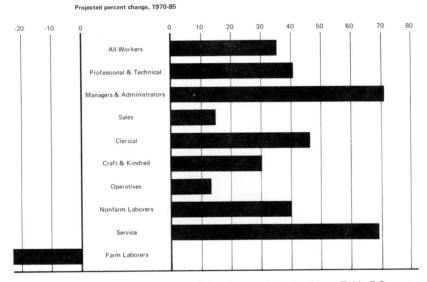

Projected percent change, 1970-85

Sources: 1977 Employment and Training Report of the President, Table E-9, page 259, and *1970 Census of Population.*

Focusing on the occupational distribution of youth employment at the beginning of the 1970s, one can find considerable variation by age, sex, and race (Table 4-2). Teenagers were clustered in clerical, service, and operative employment, accounting for 44.5 percent of their total employment. Young adults, in turn, 20 to 24 years of age were also grouped in clerical and operative occupations, but with substantial numbers in professional and technical employment. The latter accounts for nearly 16 percent of this group's employment. Nearly half of the young women in both age groups were in clerical occupations, whereas young men were more evenly distributed, with one out of four employed as operatives.

Among teenagers and young adults, important differences in the occupational distribution of nonwhites and whites can be found. Nonwhites and whites have basically the same occupational distribution as teenagers, but differences emerge in the cross section among young adults. Reflecting in part differences in education, whites hold a much larger share of professional and technical employment than young blacks. As young adults, blacks continue to be concentrated in service employment, whereas whites shift from service employment to white-collar occupations. For whatever reasons, it appears that blacks fail as young adults to move into white-collar occupations in the same proportions as young whites.

These patterns are significant because they show many youths in occupations expected to grow at above average rates through 1985. But equally important is the fact that not all youths will benefit proportionately from this growth. The concentration of young blacks in slow-growth blue-collar employment, for example, will adversely affect their employment in the mid-1980s unless occupational upgrading occurs. Without such intervention, the changing economy of the 1980s will contribute to the structural unemployment of youth.

Table 4-2. Occupational Distribution of Employment for Youth 16-19 by Sex and Race, 1970

Occupational group	Total	Male	Female	Nonwhite	White
Number	5,252,299	2,944,815	2,307,484	441,275	4,811,024
Percent distribution	100.0	100.0	100.0	100.0	100.0
Professional and technical	3.3	3.2	3.6	3.3	3.3
Managers and administrators, except farm	0.9	1.2	0.5	0.1	1.0
Sales workers	9.8	7.7	12.5	4.9	10.2
Clerical workers	25.2	10.1	44.5	25.5	25.2
Craft and kindred	5.8	9.7	0.9	5.6	5.9
Operatives	16.8	23.3	8.5	18.9	16.6
Nonfarm laborers	12.1	20.4	1.4	12.1	12.1
Service workers	22.5	18.8	27.2	26.2	22.1
Farmers and farm laborers	3.5	5.6	0.8	3.5	3.5

Source: 1970 Census of the Population.

Youth Unemployment Projections

It is possible to explore the impact on youth unemployment of the changing occupational structure in the nation, if one assumes there will be no aggregate shifts between occupations through 1985. While it is unlikely that occupational shares held by youths in 1970 will persist to 1985, the assumption that age groups remain constant within occupational categories provides a limiting case to demonstrate the importance of occupational mobility for youths. Briefly, with this approach the 1970 share of total employment in each occupation is determined by age group, race, and sex. These shares are then applied to the employment projections by occupation for 1985 and summed over all occupations (Table 4-3). This procedure yields employment estimates for teenagers and young adults by race and sex, based upon the 1970 occupational distribution and employment projections for 1985. The amount of unemployment can also be projected, along with unemployment rates (Table 4-4). Within this limiting case, the results show that black youth in 1985 will account for nearly one out of three unemployed teenagers and four out of ten unemployed young adults. This demonstrates the importance of expanding black employment opportunities, including the movement of black youth into occupations with above average growth rates.

The projections shown in Table 4-4 offer other interesting insights concerning youth unemployment in the 1980s. Because the share of total youth employment held by blacks in 1985 will naturally increase along with the increase in their share of the total civilian labor force, the projected black youth unemployment rate will be somewhat lower, while the rate for white youth will be somewhat higher. The number of young adults during this period will be inflated by the last of the postwar baby boom population. Unless this age group's share of total employment rises in proportion to their share of the civilian labor force, the young adult unemployment rate will surpass that for teenagers. The teenage unemployment rate, in contrast, will be reduced substantially from that of the present as a consequence of the declining number of new labor force entrants. With the relative increase of young

58

Occupational group	Total	Male	Female	Nonwhite	White
Table 4-3. Occupational Distribution of Employment for Youth 20-24 by Sex and Race, 1970					
Number	9,341,086	4,984,174	4,356,912	946,588	8,430,347
Percent distribution	100.0	100.0	100.0	100.0	100.0
Professional and technical	15.9	14.4	17.7	8.2	16.7
Managers and administrators, except farm	3.3	4.9	1.6	1.3	3.5
Sales workers	5.7	6.3	5.0	2.9	6.0
Clerical workers	27.8	11.2	46.8	25.3	28.0
Craft and kindred	10.6	18.7	1.2	7.4	10.9
Operatives	17.9	24.2	10.8	25.7	17.0
Nonfarm laborers	5.3	9.2	0.8	8.5	4.9
Service workers	11.7	8.1	15.8	18.5	11.1
Farmers and farm laborers	1.8	2.9	0.4	2.2	1.8

Source: 1970 Census of the Population.

Table 4-4. 1985 Employment Projections for Youths, 16 to 24 Years of Age, by Occupation, Based Upon the 1970 Youth Occupational Distribution by Sex and Race (thousands)

Occupation	Projected total employment requirements	Projected employment 16-19 years of age			Projected employment 20-24 years of age		
		Total	Female	Nonwhite	Total	Female	Nonwhite
Professional or technical workers	16,000	248	117	21	2,099	1,085	109
Managers and administrators, except farm	10,900	84	21	4	533	117	21
Sales workers	6,300	589	330	25	608	248	31
Clerical workers	20,100	1,936	1,502	165	3,797	2,981	350
Craft and kindred workers	13,800	399	28	28	1,283	69	91
Operatives	15,200	997	222	94	1,892	529	274
Nonfarm laborers	4,800	887	47	75	695	51	113
Service workers	14,600	1,999	1,063	196	1,843	1,162	251
Farmers and farm laborers	1,900	149	16	13	132	15	9
Total	103,400	7,288	3,346	621	12,882	6,257	1,250

Source: Projected total employment requirements by occupation are from Table E-9, p. 259, 1977 Employment and Training Report of the President. Projected employment for youth is derived by multiplying total employment requirements by age, sex, cohort share to 1970 total employment by occupation.

Table 4-5. Youth Unemployment Projections for 1985 Based Upon the 1970 Youth Occupational Distribution by Age, Sex, and Race

(thousands)

Age/Sex	Civilian labor force participation rate	Civilian non-institutional population	Civilian labor force	Employed	Unemployed	Unemployment rates
	(1)	(2)	(3)	(4)	(3)-(4) = (5)	(5)/(3) = (6)
16-19 years:	57.2	13,388	7,943	7,288	655	8.2
Males	60.9	6,870	4,181	3,942	239	5.7
Females	53.6	7,018	3,762	3,346	416	11.1
Nonwhites	36.5	2,383	869	621	248	28.5
Whites	61.5	11,505	7,074	6,667	407	5.8
20-24 years:	77.5	19,501	15,123	12,882	2,241	14.8
Males	83.0	9,386	7,790	6,625	1,165	15.0
Females	72.5	10,115	7,333	6,257	1,076	14.7
Nonwhites	68.6	3,087	2,117	1,250	867	40.9
Whites	79.2	16,415	13,007	11,632	1,375	10.6

Sources: Civilian labor force participation rates and civilian labor force estimates for males and females are from Howard N. Fullerton and Paul O. Flaim, "New Labor Force Projections to 1990," *Monthly Labor Review*, December 1976. Reprinted as Special L.F. Report No. 197. Estimates of these measures by race are from unpublished estimates prepared by Bureau of Labor Statistics for Office of the Assistant Secretary of Policy Evaluation and Research, U.S. Department of Labor, 1977.

Employment projections are derived by multiplying the occupational employment requirements for 1985 (Table E-9, p. 259, *1977 Employment and Training Report of the President*) by the age-sex-race cohort share of total employment by occupation in 1970 and summing. The occupational employment requirements for 1985 are based upon a 4.8 percent unemployment rate.

adults in relation to teenagers, however, teenagers will doubtless find increasing competition for jobs from their older counterparts. The substitution of young adults for teenagers, therefore, can be expected to maintain teenage unemployment rates above those of young adults. For young men and women, unemployment relationships in the 1980s will remain basically unchanged.

Similar projections to those included in Table 4-4 might be made by linear extrapolation of the postwar trends in youth occupational shares. However, biased upward by the influx of youths into the labor force during the 1960s, these trends would clearly overstate the expected employment of youths in the 1980s. Not only will the youth labor force share have reversed its trend upward by this time, by 1985 it will have returned to its 1970 level. As suggested below, several intervening factors will influence these trends in the decade ahead, thus reducing the value of further extrapolation.

Prospects for Youth Employment

Whereas the share of youth employment held by blacks in the mid-1980s is likely to increase along with their relative number in the civilian labor force, the actual number of jobs open to youths, black and white, will depend upon a host of factors. Included among these are economic growth and the adult unemployment rate, the relative size of the adult labor force, the duration of education, the extent of competition for youth jobs from other labor force groups, the size of the military, and the ability of youth to move into occupations marked by above average growth.

The BLS employment projections for 1985 are based upon an unemployment rate of 4.8 percent. Unemployment among those 16 years of age and over, however, is currently hovering around 7 percent. If unemployment rates persist at this level through 1985, employment will decline by 2.4 million jobs. The impact of this would rest heavily upon youths, particularly black youths, and would further exacerbate the youth unemployment problem. Accordingly, full employment policies will play an active role in determining the level of youth unemployment in the 1980s.

Youths 16 to 24 years of age are expected to represent 21.2 percent of all labor force participants 16 years of age and older in 1985, approximately the same as in 1970, 21.6 percent. The distribution of young people in relation to adults in the civilian labor force of 1985 is an important indicator of whether youth are likely to maintain the same share of employment held in 1970. If the relative number of youths has fallen, for example, as it will have by the end of the 1980s, their share of total employment in all likelihood will fall below that projected in Table 4-3, increasing the projected level of youth unemployment for 1985.

Expected changes in the age, sex, and race composition of the youth labor force will also affect the youth share of total employment. As the groups with above average unemployment, such as young women and blacks, increase, this will serve to reduce the youth employment share. This would be offset in part or in total, however, by the relative increase of young adults whose unemployment rates historically have been lower than those of teenagers.

The duration of schooling can be added to those factors expected to affect youth employment in the decade ahead. Although more and more youth are combining schooling and work, the duration of schooling tends to postpone full-time entry into the labor force. Rising levels of education in the postwar period have thus served to absorb many youths who might otherwise have been searching for work earlier. In view of recent evidence indicating lower economic returns to postsecondary education, this trend may weaken, leading to more youths entering the labor market earlier and thereby increasing youth employment and possibly unemployment.

Clearly, changes in national defense needs could radically alter the youth employment picture. During the height of the Vietnam War, the military absorbed an annual average of over 2.2 million youths 18 to 24 years of age. In 1976, the volunteer armed forces employed only half this number. In the event of another military crisis, youth employment would be increased substantially.

Also affecting the youth share of total employment is the extent of competition for youth jobs from other labor force groups. Youth will face increased competition from women, whose labor force participation rates will continue to climb in the 1980s. In addition, an emerging source of competition can be found among older workers. Increasing in number, older workers will perhaps find the part-time employment sought by many teenagers an attractive means of supplementing retirement income and easing economic pressures created by inflation. Finally, the estimated 6 to 12 million undocumented aliens in the country, a group that works "hard and scared," will compete for the approximately 20 million youth jobs projected for 1985.

Whatever the effect of the above factors on youth employment, a notable factor remaining is the ability of youths to move into those occupations experiencing above average growth. Traditional blue-collar jobs held by the young are diminishing in importance. The ability of young people to find new jobs in growth sectors of the economy will determine, in large part, the effect of the changing economy upon youth unemployment in the 1980s. Trends described in Chapter 2 suggest that youths have been moving into growth occupations, but not rapidly enough to reduce the now familiar two-to-one ratio of youths to total unemployment. The present outlook is for youth unemployment to improve only in accord with improvement in the overall unemployment rate. Reduction of the relative levels of youth unemployment, at least to 1985, would appear to require more effective policy action than has been evident in the past.

THE TRANSITION FROM SCHOOL TO WORK

By
Wayne Stevenson

The American youth unemployment experience and the outlook for the decade ahead have been described in preceding chapters. From this description, one might conclude that youth unemployment will not yield to policies of economic stimulation alone, although these policies are an important condition for improvement. To a large degree, the problem is structural in nature, deeply rooted in the conditions affecting the age structure of the population, the transition from school to work, the changing structure of the national economy, and the deterioration of urban labor markets. Underlying these are racial overtones that compound the problem.

This chapter focuses on the transition from school to work and the way in which the transition correlates with early labor market experiences. Using longitudinal data from a national sample of young men and women 16 to 19 years of age, one sees that a correlation indeed exists between the early labor market experience of these youths and the characteristics of home, community, and school. Providing additional insight into the youth unemployment experience, this chapter serves as a foundation for the one to follow which examines the same panel of youths seven years later and the relationship between early labor market experience and subsequent employment experience.

Longitudinal data show the transition from school to work to be a gradual process rather than an abrupt movement into the labor force when school is completed. The high incidence of unemployment experienced by youth as teenagers and later as young adults is seen as part of the transition process, with entry-level jobs associated with high turnover and little job security. The relationship of age, sex, and race to the likelihood of youth unemployment has already been discussed. In the sections to follow, education, family background, and other measures of personal characteristics and environment are found to be related in a predictable way to a variety of measures of early labor market experience.

Approach to the Problem

The movement of youth between school and work has been described using cross section data from the Current Population Surveys. These data reveal that most individuals succeed in making the school-to-work transition. Unemployment rates are highest among those 16 to 17 years of age and decline thereafter until age 65. As individuals age and become more firmly attached to the work force, the jobless rate declines, suggesting that only a fraction fail to make the switch.

Cross section data, however, fail to allow one to follow an individual through the period of transition from school to work so that relationships at two or more points in time can be determined. The relationship between pre-labor market and early labor market experience, as well as subsequent experience, can be determined only if a group of individuals is followed through time. For example, it would be important to know whether prime age workers who are unemployed or underemployed are the same individuals who incurred these experiences when they were young. Longitudinal data make this possible.

Analyses in this chapter and the next are based on data from the National Longitudinal Surveys (NLS).[1] These surveys constitute a 10-year longitudinal study of the labor market experience of four subsets of the U.S. noninstitutionalized civilian population: men 45 to 59 years of age, women 30 to 44 years of age, and young men and women 14 to 24 years of age. For each of these cohorts, a national probability sample of approximately 5,000 respondents was drawn by the Bureau of the Census. The analysis presented here is based upon data for 16- to 19-year-olds, collected over a span of seven years, beginning in 1966 for the young men and 1968 for the young women.

NLS data were designed to measure sources of variation in the labor market experiences of each cohort. The data, therefore, include a broad sampling of economic, social, and attitudinal characteristics of the youth population. Labor force concepts used are consistent with those of the Current Population Survey. To provide enough observations for racial comparisons, blacks were oversampled on a three to one ratio. The transition from school to work is examined with these data, using multiple regression analysis and analysis of variance techniques.

School Enrollment and Labor Force Participation

Aside from recreation and family responsibilities, the major activity of most pre-teenagers is school. On the other hand, for those over 24 years of age, the dominant activity is work. For most individuals, the transition from school to work takes place in the intervening years. Some make the change abruptly, with a rapid and definite passage from school to work. Others gradually move between school and part-time summer work to full-time employment. Many fluctuate unpredictably between school and work, between employment and unemployment, and in and out of the labor market before finding a permanent place in the labor force, if indeed they ever do. Regardless of when or how quickly the change is made, the period of transition from school to work is marked by uncertainty. Whether they are successfully assimilated by the labor force depends to a great extent on what transpires during these critical years.

The frequently held belief that meaningful labor force participation begins upon the completion of school is ill-founded. As shown in Chapter 3, it is increasingly true that new labor force entrants ease into the labor market by combining work with school before terminating their education. The way in which age influences the decision regarding school and labor force participation is shown in Figures 5-1 and 5-2. It can be seen that during the initial survey year about 65 percent of all teenagers 16 to 19 years old were enrolled in school. At the same time, 45 percent of the females and 70 percent of the males were labor force participants and unemployment rates were rather high, particularly for blacks and females.

The patterns change rapidly with age, however. Labor force participation rises as school enrollment declines. By the time these groups become young adults 20 to 23 years of age, school enrollment is below 20 percent—except for white males, 28 percent of whom are still in school. By the final survey year, when the respondents range in age from 23 to 26, the transition from school to work is complete for most. Only about 10 percent remain in school, and labor force participation rates approach those typically associated with adult workers. While unemployment rates remain uncomfortably high for blacks and females, they are below earlier levels and have dropped to three percent for white males.

These figures demonstrate that, as a group, young workers enter the labor force gradually rather than abruptly upon the completion of school. A period of trial and experimentation precedes complete assimilation into the labor force. Large numbers of teenagers and young adults combine school and work before completing the transition. This process is made possible largely through the opportunity for part-time employment.

Figure 5-1. Civilian Labor Force Participation, School Enrollment, and Unemployment Rates for Aging Cohort of Males Who Were 16-19 Years of Age in 1966

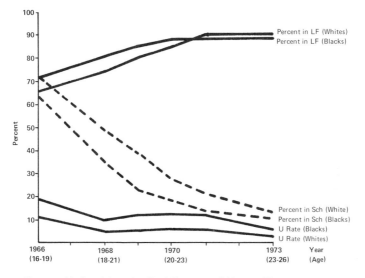

Source: National Longitudinal Surveys of Young Men.

Figure 5-2. Civilian Labor Force Participation, School Enrollment and Unemployment Rates for Aging Cohort of Females Who Were 16-19 Years of Age

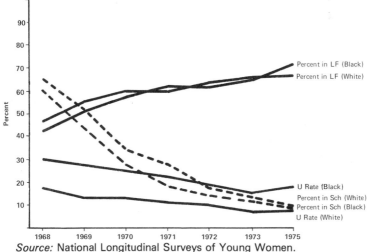

Source: National Longitudinal Surveys of Young Women.

69

Among all employed teenagers in the initial survey years who were enrolled in school, 87 percent held part-time jobs. The incidence of part-time employment for out-of-school youth was considerably lower, 11 percent. Table 5-1 shows the proportion of youths in part-time employment declining with age. As young adults, ages 20 to 23, most work full time, with only 17 percent in part-time employment.

Table 5-1. Percent of Youth Employed Part Time, by Sex, Age, Race, Survey Year, and Age of Cohort

Cohort race and sex	Survey Year and Age of Cohort		
	First survey yr. 16 to 19	Third survey yr. 18 to 21	Fifth survey yr. 20 to 23
Young men:			
White	54	29	15
Black	44	19	12
Young women:			
White	54	29	21
Black	49	24	19
TOTAL	52	27	17

Source: National Longitudinal Surveys.

Entry-Level Jobs

It is difficult to determine when an individual actually enters the labor market. Work often starts as low-paying, part-time work during the summers, on weekends, or after school. For many, as they approach the end of school, job search intensifies. At this time, labor force participation takes on a new dimension, with work replacing school as the dominant activity for those who manage to secure employment. This might be the logical point at which an individual is considered to have fully entered the labor market. Entry-level jobs secured at this time differ by industry and occupation from jobs held during high school and those of mature workers.

As part of the NLS study, respondents were asked to provide information on their first job after leaving school. Such information was supplied by 2,301 of the males and by 2,153 of the females. Young men and women were also asked the occupation and industry of the last job they held while still in high school. Tables 5-2 and 5-3 compare industry and occupational distributions of all workers with youth entry-level and high school jobs. The data show that two-thirds of the men and four-fifths of the women were employed as students in wholesale and retail trade, or in services and recreation. By contrast, the distribution of entry-level employment more nearly reflects the industry distribution of all workers. As the cohort moves from high school jobs to entry-level jobs, there is a shift away from wholesale and retail trade and toward manufacturing, construction, and public administration.

Blacks are far more likely to enter the labor force in agricultural and service employment than their white counterparts. In comparison to men, women, especially white women, are more likely to find their first post-school employment in finance, insurance, and services. Men are more likely to begin their careers in construction and manufacturing. Some of these differences are no doubt due to age and years of school completed at time of entry, for which there is no attempt to control in this analysis. Many of these patterns persist into the years as adult workers.

Comparing the occupational distributions, one can see that high school and entry-level jobs tend to be in low-skill occupations. Nearly 60 percent of early jobs among males are as laborers and operatives. The highest concentrations of women are in service, clerical, and sales work. Among women, there are some distinct racial differences. Black women are less likely than white women to begin in sales work, but more likely to be in service occupations, particularly as private household workers.

Other characteristics of entry-level jobs were obtained in the surveys. Within their respective occupational groups, 45 percent of all respondents indicated they were employed at the lowest or next to lowest occupational level. Of those working with tools or

Table 5-2. Last High School and Entry-Level Employment of Males by Industry and Occupation (percent distribution)

Industry	Whites		Blacks		Males & females 16 years old and over[c]
	Last job in high school[a]	Entry-level job[b]	Last job in high school[a]	Entry-level job[b]	
TOTAL	100.0	100.0	100.0	100.0	100.0
Agriculture, forestry, and fisheries	14.8	10.1	9.7	19.2	4.2
Mining	0.1	0.6	0.0	0.3	0.8
Construction	5.0	10.7	5.4	9.4	4.6
Manufacturing	9.3	27.8	2.3	22.1	25.1
Transportation, communication	2.0	4.2	6.7	3.4	5.6
Wholesale/retail trade	47.9	26.4	36.9	20.4	19.5
Finance, insurance, and real estate	0.7	2.0	0.4	1.7	4.8
Services and recreation	17.1	13.4	29.4	18.8	15.1
Public administration	0.5	2.3	0.9	2.2	16.3
Others	0.0	1.8	0.0	0.7	3.8

Occupation					Males, 16 years old and over[c]
Professional and technical workers	2.3	10.5	2.3	2.2	14.0
Managers and proprietors	1.1	3.8	0.2	0.5	14.2
Clerical workers	7.9	8.6	6.3	7.0	7.1
Sales workers	13.9	5.1	7.7	1.7	5.6
Craft and kindred workers	6.7	12.2	5.4	6.9	20.1
Operatives	19.5	28.6	19.2	21.9	19.6
Private household workers	0.2	0.0	0.9	0.0	0.1
Service workers	15.5	4.8	26.9	17.1	6.6
Farm owners and managers	0.7	1.3	0.0	0.7	3.4
Farm laborers	12.5	7.0	8.8	15.9	1.9
Non-farm laborers	15.5	15.5	4.8	23.6	7.3
Others	0.0	1.9	0.0	0.7	—

[a]Based on National Longitudinal Surveys responses by 2,060 males.

[b]Based on National Longitudinal Surveys responses by 2,301 males.

[c]Based on 1970 figures reported in the 1977 Employment and Training Report of the President. Tables A-15 and C-1.

Table 5-3. Last High School and Entry-Level Employment of Females by Industry and Occupation (percent distribution)

Industry	Whites		Blacks		Males & females 16 years old and over[c]
	Last job in high school[a]	Entry-level job[b]	Last job in high school[a]	Entry-level job[b]	
TOTAL	100.0	100.0	100.0	100.0	100.0
Agriculture, forestry, and fisheries	1.9	1.1	6.3	6.0	4.2
Mining	0.0	0.2	0.0	0.0	0.8
Construction	0.1	0.8	0.0	0.2	4.6
Manufacturing	5.9	20.1	2.8	15.0	25.1
Transportation and communication	1.8	5.2	4.0	2.7	5.6
Wholesale/retail trade	54.4	28.6	25.0	19.1	19.5
Finance, insurance, and real estate	3.1	9.7	1.1	2.5	4.8
Services and recreation	32.0	30.2	55.1	49.9	15.1
Public administration	0.7	4.0	5.7	4.8	16.3
Others	0.0	0.0	0.0	0.0	3.8

74

Occupation					Females, 16 years old & over[c]
Professional and technical workers	2.6	9.5	2.3	3.5	14.5
Managers and proprietors	0.4	1.0	0.0	0.2	4.5
Clerical workers	31.5	42.7	31.4	24.6	34.5
Sales workers	21.5	8.0	8.0	3.4	7.0
Craft and kindred workers	0.3	0.8	0.0	0.9	1.1
Operatives	2.9	14.3	4.0	17.0	14.5
Private household workers	10.0	3.9	20.0	17.0	5.1
Service workers	29.0	18.5	27.4	26.9	16.5
Farm owners and managers	0.0	0.0	0.0	0.0	0.3
Farm laborers	0.9	0.8	6.3	6.0	1.5
Non-farm laborers	0.9	0.6	0.6	0.7	0.5
Others	0.0	0.0	0.0	0.0	—

[a]Based on National Longitudinal Surveys responses by 851 females.

[b]Based on National Longitudinal Surveys responses by 2,153 females.

[c]Based on 1970 figures reported in the 1977 Employment and Training Report of the President, Tables A-15 and C-1.

75

machines on their first job, 87 percent said that no specialized training was required, and more than two-thirds of those in sales work claimed no special knowledge of the products sold. Approximately 90 percent were employed by private firms and, for those no longer employed in their first job, over 65 percent had left of their own accord.

Examination of industry, occupation, and other characteristics of entry-level jobs reveals that they tend to be associated with low pay, high turnover, and high unemployment. In addition, they are in industries and occupations where the incidence of part-time work is rather high. For example, while 27 percent of all employment in services and wholesale and retail trade is part time, the corresponding proportion in manufacturing and public administration is six percent. The proportion of all employment which is part time is about 16 percent.

Thus high school employment, along with employment in first jobs held upon leaving school, tends to be "secondary" jobs, with limited opportunities for advancement or permanence. Few, if any, job-related skills are required, and the jobs can be learned rapidly. Such work can be expected to pay little more than the minimum wage and provide little in the way of job-related skills that can be used on other jobs. So-called primary jobs that offer good pay and security are seldom found immediately after high school graduation. Nevertheless, this does not reduce the value of secondary jobs as both developers and demonstrators of work attitudes and work habits which are important skills in themselves.

Early Labor Market Success

As discussed earlier, age, race, and sex are major determinants of school enrollment status, labor force participation and, in particular, unemployment. But there are other indicators of labor market activity and early labor market success. Employment experiences differ in terms of wages, hours and weeks worked, stability, and total remuneration over the year. Table 5-4 shows

Table 5-4. Labor Market Experience of 16- to 19-Year Olds by Race, Sex, and School Enrollment Status: 1966 for Young Men and 1968 for Young Women

Teenage labor market experience	In school				Out of school			
	White		Black		White		Black	
	Male	Female	Male	Female	Male	Female	Male	Female
Survey week:								
Percent in labor force	57.1	37.9	59.2	33.7	92.2	63.3	90.6	56.8
Percent of labor force employed	85.0	81.4	76.5	68.5	94.3	83.9	87.0	71.6
Hours worked per week	18.3	13.9	18.6	14.0	41.6	36.0	39.2	35.6
Percent of labor force unemployed	15.0	18.6	23.5	31.5	5.7	16.1	13.0	28.4
Current or last job:								
Wages per hour (dollars)	1.50	1.23	1.39	1.21	1.91	1.57	1.78	1.42
Occupational status	21.8	28.5	16.5	23.2	21.9	33.5	15.9	26.3
Past year:								
Weeks worked	24.6	15.2	21.2	11.1	37.2	22.9	33.8	17.5
Weeks unemployed	1.9	5.8	2.7	8.2	2.0	6.7	3.2	7.5
Percent with 2 or more spells of unemployment	33.1	24.7	33.8	27.9	43.2	21.0	45.3	33.9
Wage and salary income (dollars)	718	307	475	214	2,234	1,165	1,440	692

Source: National Longitudinal Surveys.

77

how these and related measures vary among different groups of teenagers represented in the NLS population.

The importance of race, sex, and school enrollment status are clearly evident. Labor force participation rates are predictably higher for out-of-school youth. Racial differences in participation rates are relatively small, but in all categories women are much less likely than men to be in the labor force. For those in the labor force, the probability of unemployment is highest among females and among blacks of either sex. Young men, however, appear to have more frequent spells of unemployment. For employed teenagers, the number of hours worked and the wages received by males are considerably above those of females. It appears that race has little impact on the number of hours worked during weeks of employment, but the number of weeks worked and the rate of pay for blacks are below those for whites. These differences combined create considerable variation in the labor market experiences of the teenagers examined.

The principal objective of labor market activity—whether stable or unstable, well paid or poorly paid—is income. Hourly wages combine with hours and weeks worked, interspersed with periods of unemployment or spells out of the labor force, to yield annual income. Income probably serves as the best summary measure of what recent labor market inactivity means in economic terms to an individual. Comparisons of wage and salary income with occupational status[2] reveal important differences for the various groups represented in Table 5-4. Higher rates of labor force participation, lower rates of unemployment, and more full-time work combine to make the annual wage and salary income of out-of-school teenagers three to four times greater than that of in-school youths. Similarly, men exhibit a greater attachment to the labor force than women, resulting in a two to one margin in earnings. While labor force participation rates differ little between blacks and whites, the overall experience of blacks in the labor force results in earnings and occupational status far below those of their white counterparts. Thus, the labor market advantage enjoyed by white men in later years is part of a pattern which begins to develop during the early years of the school-to-work transition.

Correlates of Early Labor Market Experience

It is evident that age plays a dominant role in determining the labor market experience of youth. Not only does labor force participation increase and unemployment decline with age, but along with a stronger attachment to the labor market come higher wages and incomes. Each year sees an increase in the average number of hours worked per week, as well as the number of weeks worked per year, until the age of 25 is reached. Around these averages, however, considerable variation exists with a variety of contributing factors. In this section, several measures reflecting the influence of home, community, and school are examined in an attempt to describe the variation in labor market activity and early labor market success.

In addition to age, race, and sex, a number of other variables are expected to affect the labor market experiences of young workers. School enrollment status and level of education are typically associated with labor market activity and earnings.[3] It was shown earlier that those out of school are more likely to be in full-time work and have a stronger attachment to their jobs and the labor market in general. Furthermore, the number of years of school completed represents one very important measure of skill accumulation and is expected to be directly related to employability and annual earnings.

One would also expect family background to have a significant impact on early labor market experiences. Previous studies suggest that while much of the influence of socioeconomic background is transmitted through the quantity and quality of education received, socioeconomic status exerts an impact of its own as well.[4] Responsibility, self-discipline, personality, and communication skills are all thought to be well developed before the age at which school attendance typically begins. In addition, the role models of parents and neighbors are considered to be quite important in establishing aspirations, attitudes toward work, and information pertinent to employment opportunities. Thus, inclusion of a socioeconomic index based upon parents' education, father's occupation, and the presence of reading materials in the home can be expected to increase the ability to explain variation in early labor market experience.[5]

Educational as well as other family background deficiencies of those from less favorable environments are expected to emerge later in the form of greater employment instability, higher unemployment, and lower earnings. Thus, both education and socioeconomic status, while related to one another, are included as explanatory variables in the analysis that follows.[6]

Marital status and place of residence are also expected to have their effect. Married workers with greater responsibilities are generally better established in their careers. This may result in greater job stability and earnings, although the flow of causation is somewhat ambiguous. Living in an urban area generally offers more opportunities for employment than living in a rural area. Living in the South, in turn, involves access to lower paying and less secure employment.

One additional variable included in the model is knowledge of the world of work. More information concerning earnings, education requirements, and other occupational characteristics are expected to be rewarded in a number of ways. Good labor market information would result in coordination between occupational aspirations and the amount and type of education received. In addition, the job search process would be more efficient, resulting in less job turnover, fewer and shorter periods of unemployment, and higher wages.

It should be mentioned, however, that the measure of labor market information employed here is closely related to several other variables.[7] It is directly related to ability as measured by IQ scores and thus provides a proxy for intelligence otherwise unavailable for most observations. It is also directly related to socioeconomic status, age, and the number of years of school completed.[8]

This is far from an exhaustive list of factors which can be expected to influence early labor market experience. Understanding the influence these variables have on labor market activity and early labor market success, however, will greatly expand understanding of the youth labor market beyond that which can be gleaned from regularly published series.[9]

Labor Force Participation and Unemployment

Two of the most important and frequently used indicators of labor market activity are the labor force participation rate and the unemployment rate. The labor force participation measure is a binary variable coded as 1 for those in the labor force and 0 for those out of the labor force. The unemployment variable is similarly defined for all labor force participants, assuming the value of 1 for those unemployed and 0 for others. Using these as dependent variables, Table 5-5 provides estimates of the likelihood of labor force participation and unemployment. The results, using multiple regression analysis, indicate the impact of the explanatory variables on these measures. Observations consist of males and females between 16 and 19 years of age.

Race, years of schooling completed, and current school enrollment status exert somewhat mixed impacts on labor force participation and unemployment. Labor force participation rates do not differ significantly between blacks and whites. Once in the labor force, however, differences arise. Blacks, and particularly black females, are more likely to be unemployed. School enrollment status demonstrates a sizable impact on both labor force participation and unemployment. Labor force participation rates are significantly higher and unemployment lower for those out of school, when other factors are constant. The years of school completed exert a less certain impact. Higher levels of schooling seem to be related to lower unemployment, but only for females is more schooling associated with significantly higher labor force participation.

Other factors demonstrating a fairly consistent relationship with labor force participation and unemployment are marital status and region of residence. After controlling for other differences,

Table 5-5. The Likelihood of Labor Force Participation and Unemployment for 16-19 Year Old Males and Females

Explanatory variables	Probability of labor force participation		Probability of unemployment[a]	
	Males	Females	Males	Females
Black	-0.76	1.69	6.69	10.83
	(0.29)	(0.58)	(2.74)***	(3.01)***
Years of school completed	-0.77	3.37	-1.99	-1.51
	(1.03)	(3.67)****	(2.96)***	(1.25)
Out of school	25.05	31.12	-4.92	-4.59
	(11.88)****	(11.14)****	(2.42)***	(1.44)*
Socioeconomic status	-0.17	-0.12	0.10	0.05
	(2.83)***	(1.90)**	(1.62)*	(0.64)
Married	19.10	-20.27	-8.93	9.31
	(4.30)****	(5.48)****	(2.54)***	(2.14)**
Lives in SMSA	0.50	6.30	4.19	-0.59
	(0.22)	(2.73)***	(2.11)**	(0.20)
Lives in non-South	6.35	11.27	0.12	4.46
	(2.78)***	(4.47)****	(0.05)	(1.38)*
Labor market knowledge	-0.00	1.58	-0.12	-2.55
	(0.00)	(2.37)***	(0.83)	(2.97)***
R^2 (adjusted)	0.11	0.12	0.03	0.04
Degrees of freedom	2,010	1,824	1,373	833
Standard error	0.44	0.47	0.34	0.40
F- value	32.58	31.31	6.22	5.06

Source: National Longitudinal Surveys.

Significance levels: 10% (*) 5% (**) 1% (***) 0.1% (****)

t-values are in parentheses.

Coefficients are multiplied by 100.

[a]Variable is defined only for those in the labor force.

labor force participation is about 19 percentage points higher for males who are married and over 20 percentage points lower for married females. Once in the labor force, the likelihood of being unemployed is lower for married males but considerably higher for married females. Marital status is clearly one of the most important correlates of teenage labor market activity.

While labor force participation rates tend to be lower in the South, region and place of residence have mixed effects on the likelihood of being unemployed once in the labor force. For males, living in an urban area appears to be related to a higher incidence of unemployment while for females living outside the South is associated with higher unemployment. Only for females does labor market knowledge seem to be correlated as expected with lower unemployment. Socioeconomic status for males and females is associated with lower labor force participation during the teenage years. Its effect upon unemployment, however, is marginal.

The question remains as to whether or not labor market activity measured during a single survey week properly characterizes youth labor market behavior or properly isolates those with chronic labor market problems. However, while not shown here, unemployment measured over the full year (i.e., the number of weeks unemployed) is related to the measures analyzed here in much the same way as survey week unemployment. Thus, those with persistent problems of unemployment are no doubt heavily represented among those counted during the survey week as unemployed.

It should be mentioned that only a small proportion of the variation in labor force participation and unemployment can be explained with these measures—about 12 percent for the probability of labor force participation and less than 5 percent for the probability of unemployment. Thus, while some general trends have been identified and discussed, the relationships are quite variable and therefore difficult to predict. A given individual—in fact, most individuals—depart substantially from these trends.

Wages, Weeks Worked, and Annual Earnings

Entering the labor force and finding employment is only one measure of early labor market success. Whether one is a teenager or an adult, employment is not generally sought for the joy of work but for the financial rewards. Once a job is found, the hourly wage in conjunction with the number of hours and weeks worked combine to determine the annual earnings of the worker. It was shown earlier that race and sex are associated with significant differences in the characteristics of teenage labor force experience. In this section the effect of other factors is taken into account.

Tables 5-6 and 5-7 show the results of multiple regression analysis designed to explain the variation in other dimensions of youth labor market success. Education, marital status, and place of residence exert the most significant and predictable effect on these measures of early labor market success. Education, measured by years of schooling completed, leads to more weeks worked per year, higher hourly wages, and significantly higher annual earnings. The returns to additional schooling, as measured in the mid-1960s, were highest among white males and lowest among blacks. Labor force activity among out of school teenagers is associated with higher pay, more weeks worked, and higher annual earnings.

After controlling for differences in education, socioeconomic status has little impact on labor market success as measured by earnings. An exception to this seems to be among white males for whom socioeconomic status is inversely related to hourly pay, number of weeks worked, and annual earnings. Interestingly enough, this relationship (which is not found among older workers) continues to hold and is of even greater magnitude when the education variables are excluded. Thus white males from more favorable backgrounds tend to be less firmly attached to the labor force (and probably more committed to full-time school) than their counterparts from low status families.

Marital status and place of residence also have a significant effect on teenage labor market activity. For white males who are

84

married, earnings are $2,300 per year greater, on the average, than for those who are not married. For blacks, being married is associated with only a $1,350 increase, on the average, in wage and salary income. For males, black and white, the earnings increment occurs through higher wages and more weeks worked. For females, being married has the opposite effect. While wages may be somewhat higher for married females, weeks worked and annual earnings decrease, although by less than the increase observed for men.

Living in a city or its suburbs seems to be associated with greater success in the teenage labor market, as measured by earnings. Living outside the South appears to be associated with higher wages, more weeks worked, and greater earnings over the year. For both women and men, labor market information is directly related to early labor market success. This is true even after controlling for differences in education, socioeconomic status and other variables known to be correlated with knowledge of the world of work.

These measures exhibit considerable variation. However, over 25 percent of the variation in the annual earnings of males and over 20 percent for females is accounted for, which is comparable to similar studies of older workers. Analysis of other measures of early labor market success yields similar results. The other measures include: number of weeks in the labor force in the past year, the Duncan Index of Socioeconomic Status, and the likelihood of experiencing any unemployment in the previous year. Only the number of weeks unemployed in the past year proved unpredictable.

Table 5-6. Determinants of Teenage Labor Market Experience by Race for Males

Explanatory variables	Whites			Blacks		
	Hourly rate of pay (cents/hour)	No. of weeks worked past year	Wage and salary income	Hourly rate of pay (cents/hour)	No. of weeks worked past year	Wage and salary income
Years of school completed	9.74 (6.30)****	0.90 (2.39)***	111.51 (4.64)****	10.60 (4.46)****	-0.53 (1.00)	56.91 (2.15)**
Out of school	21.18 (5.09)****	9.30 (9.29)****	668.35 (10.51)****	24.35 (3.39)****	7.19 (4.29)****	540.59 (6.47)****
Socioeconomic status	-0.20 (1.73)**	-0.05 (1.92)**	-5.45 (3.06)***	0.32 (1.53)*	-0.00 (0.00)	-0.59 (0.23)
Married	53.47 (6.73)****	11.53 (5.57)****	2,306.50 (17.27)****	30.41 (2.11)**	17.59 (4.77)****	1,357.17 (7.33)****
Living in SMSA	8.61 (2.13)**	-3.71 (3.81)****	51.59 (0.83)	11.19 (1.38)*	-4.02 (2.12)**	103.84 (1.10)
Living in non-South	25.91 (5.91)****	1.89 (1.78)**	183.40 (2.72)***	31.36 (4.05)****	1.34 (0.67)	246.92 (2.48)***
Labor market knowledge	0.22 (0.67)	0.10 (1.27)	12.52 (2.51)***	-0.22 (0.42)	0.28 (2.32)**	18.61 (3.13)****

R² (adjusted)	0.14	0.12	0.29	0.19	0.09	0.25
Degrees of freedom	1,137	1,451	1,429	401	548	535
Standard error	64.33	17.69	1,116.00	64.65	18.01	888.35
F- value	28.57	28.62	85.77	14.87	2.56	26.46

Source: National Longitudinal Surveys.

Significance levels: 10% (*) 5% (**) 1% (***) 0.1% (****)

t-values are in parentheses.

Table 5-7. Determinants of Teenage Labor Market Experience by Race for Females

Explanatory variables	Whites			Blacks		
	Hourly rate of pay (cents/hour)	No. of weeks worked past year	Wage and salary income	Hourly rate of pay (cents/hour)	No. of weeks worked past year	Wage and salary income
Years of school completed	12.68 (7.00)****	1.93 (4.44)****	161.19 (7.67)****	10.93 (4.89)****	1.00 (1.84)**	65.80 (3.52)****
Out of school	30.82 (6.43)****	9.90 (7.63)****	892.42 (14.23)****	11.08 (1.82)**	8.07 (4.68)****	462.46 (7.80)****
Socioeconomic status	0.01 (0.05)	-0.03 (1.18)	-1.53 (1.13)	0.18 (0.98)	0.02 (0.46)	0.95 (0.64)
Married	0.06 (0.00)	-7.18 (4.34)****	-272.58 (3.41)****	16.48 (1.90)**	-1.56 (0.63)	-73.07 (0.86)
Living in SMSA	15.67 (3.91)****	1.54 (1.53)*	148.78 (3.06)***	-5.39 (0.81)	0.09 (0.05)	29.18 (0.50)
Living in non-South	8.73 (1.87)**	4.50 (4.05)****	107.47 (2.01)**	26.61 (4.11)****	0.19 (0.11)	145.59 (2.37)***
Labor market knowledge	1.90 (1.33)*	0.96 (2.92)***	51.65 (3.25)****	3.90 (2.63)***	0.45 (1.20)	20.72 (1.63)*

R² (adjusted)	0.18	0.11	0.26	0.30	0.06	0.20
Degrees of freedom	776	1,288	1,283	237	524	520
Standard error	54.37	17.65	849.31	42.82	16.57	566.13
F- value	25.01	24.42	65.19	15.93	5.80	20.10

Source: National Longitudinal Surveys.
Significance levels: 10% (*) 5% (**) 1% (***) 0.1% (****)
t-values in parentheses.

Conclusions

In addition to confirming youth labor market characteristics suggested earlier by examination of cross section data, the longitudinal analysis of this chapter has provided additional information about the school-to-work transition and related youth employment problems. It has been shown that, as a group, teenagers combine school and work activities before entering the labor force as full-time workers or job seekers. This period is associated with a fairly high incidence of unemployment, the probability of joblessness being closely associated with a number of identifiable characteristics.

Other measures of teenage work experience were also shown to be related to personal and environmental characteristics. Blacks, women, and youth living in the South or in rural areas can be expected to fare the worst. In the chapter to follow it is shown that the labor market experience during the period of transition has a long-run effect on employability and income. Those individuals experiencing chronic problems as young workers can be expected to have trouble later on. That finding makes the observations of this chapter all the more important.

NOTES

1. Herbert Parnes, *The National Longitudinal Surveys* (Columbus, Ohio: Center for Human Resources Research, 1974).

2. As a measure of occupational status the Duncan Index is used. For a description of this index, see Otis Dudley Duncan, "A Socioeconomic Index for All Occupations" in Albert J. Reiss, *et al., Occupations and Social Status* (New York: Free Press of Glencoe, 1961), pp. 109-138.

3. G. S. Becker, *Human Capital: A Theoretical and Empirical Analysis with Special Reference to Education* (National Bureau of Economic Research, 1964); and Giora Hanoch, "An Economic Analysis of Earnings and Schooling," *Journal of Human Resources* (Summer 1967).

4. James Coleman, "Equal Schools or Equal Students," *The Public Interest* (Summer 1966); Russell Hill and Frank Stafford, "Allocation of Time to Preschool Children and Educational Opportunity," *Journal of Human Resources* (Summer 1974); and Paul Taubman, "Earnings, Education, Genetics, and Environment," *Journal of Human Resources* (Fall 1976); and Christopher Jencks, *et al., Inequality: A Reassessment of the Effect of Family and Schooling in America* (New York: Basic Books, 1972).

5. Herbert Parnes, *The National Longitudinal Surveys;* and Andrew Kohen, *Determinants of Early Labor Market Success Among Young Men: Race, Ability, Quantity and Quality of Schooling* (Columbus, Ohio: Center for Human Resources Research, 1973).

6. In the samples of teenagers analyzed here, the correlation between years of school completed and socioeconomic status is 0.52 for males and 0.43 for females. Similarly, those from less favorable backgrounds are more likely to be out of school. This multicollinearity must be kept in mind when interpreting the results which follow.

7. Herbert Parnes and Andrew Kohen, "Occupational Information and Labor Market Status: The Case of Young Men," *Journal of Human Resources* (Winter 1975).

8. Zero-order correlations with IQ, age, education, and socioeconomic status are respectively .44, .23, .52, .54. Because of the correlations with other explanatory variables, this variable was included with some reluctance, although models including and excluding labor market information generate nearly identical results.

9. The variables discussed here do not exhaust all of those investigated as part of this analysis. Measures of IQ score, regional unemployment, school quality, perception of discrimination, health limitations, public/private classification of job, and some attitudinal measures were among others tested. The results in most cases were quite variable, making inferences difficult.

THE RELATIONSHIP BETWEEN EARLY WORK EXPERIENCE AND FUTURE EMPLOYABILITY

By
Wayne Stevenson

While youth unemployment is roughly three times the overall rate for adults, it tends to be of shorter duration and concentrated among labor force entrants and reentrants. More than a third of all unemployed teenagers have never worked and another third are returning to the labor force after an interruption (most often to attend school full time). When job losers alone are considered, teenage unemployment rates are only slightly higher than the rate for older workers. Similarly, when just long term unemployment of 15 weeks or more is considered, teenage unemployment rates are much closer to overall rates. The probability of experiencing unemployment is significantly lower for males who are married and have assumed family responsibilities. In fact, the unemployment rate for young heads of households is about half that for comparable youths.

One major aspect of youth unemployment is that the situation improves substantially as individuals age. When workers reach the age of 25, labor force participation rises, work becomes predominantly full time and, most important, unemployment rates fall. This frequently leads to the conclusion that teenage unemployment is a transitory problem experienced by most and not greatly hindering successful assimilation into the labor force. Theory and intuition suggest, however, that to be frequently unemployed and otherwise to have a poor labor market experience during the early years has a deleterious effect later on, and that periods of unemployment represent loss of work experience, information, and skills and may have injurious effects on attitudes toward work. Furthermore, prospective employers view periods out of school and out of the labor force with great concern, creating a demand side barrier to employment for those with unfavorable early experiences. If this is true, teenage unemployment is more than a short term problem and its consequences may lead to long term problems of employability and earning capacity.

This chapter examines the long-run consequences of the youth labor market experience by following the two cohorts of young men and women who were teenagers 16 to 19 years of age in the initial National Longitudinal Surveys through seven years to young adulthood. When employment patterns of the over 1,500 young men and women are tracked over time, patterns observed among adult workers are seen to emerge. Of primary importance is the finding that early labor market experiences are related to subsequent measures of labor market success. Not only does labor market activity help to identify a potential target group of individuals who are likely to have trouble later on, but after controlling for a number of personal characteristics, youth labor force status is seen to exert an impact of its own on subsequent experiences.

Changing Employment Patterns

It has already been shown that the transition from school to work takes place gradually, with school enrollment falling off and full-time labor force participation increasing with age. Jobs held during school tend to be part time and require little skill or training. The first jobs held after leaving school also tend to be relatively low-paying positions that require little experience. Although distribution of employment in entry-level positions shows some shift from that of the last job held in school, entry-level positions still tend to be concentrated in occupations and industries that show a high percentage of part-time workers and rapid turnover with little long term stability. It remains to be seen how workers move up the job ladder into more permanent positions.

Figures 6-1 and 6-2 show the distribution of employment by occupation and industry for aging cohorts of males and females. The groups begin as teenagers, 16 to 19 years of age, in the initial survey year and are in their mid-twenties, 23 to 26, by the final survey. The patterns differ significantly for young men and young women. At all ages, women are more likely to be employed as clerical and service workers. Over two-thirds of all teenage women are found in these categories. The passage of time finds the proportion employed in services declining rapidly, although it remains high for clerical workers. Young men, on the other hand, are far less likely to be found in clerical employment. Instead, their employment is clustered in laborer, operative, and service occupations. With the passage of time, young men move out of these positions and show gains in professional occupations.

Comparing distributions by industry, differences and changes over time are less pronounced. Men are more likely to find work in construction and manufacturing, while 40 percent of the women are employed in services and recreation. Of these women, about 70 percent are in professional services. As the cohorts age, employment declines in wholesale and retail trade as well as agriculture, forestry, and mining. The most substantial gains with age are found in manufacturing, with smaller shifts toward public administration, transportation, communication, and finance.

However, the figures do not show the racial differences that exist. Whether male or female, blacks remain heavily concentrated in service and unskilled laborer occupations, consistent with

Figure 6-1. Percentage Distribution of Employment by Occupation for Aging Cohorts of Males and Females

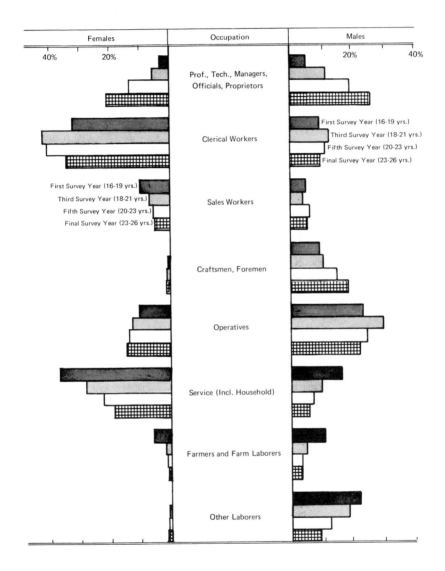

Source: National Longitudinal Surveys of Young Men and Young Women.

Figure 6-2. Percentage Distribution of Employment by Industry for Aging Cohorts of Males and Females

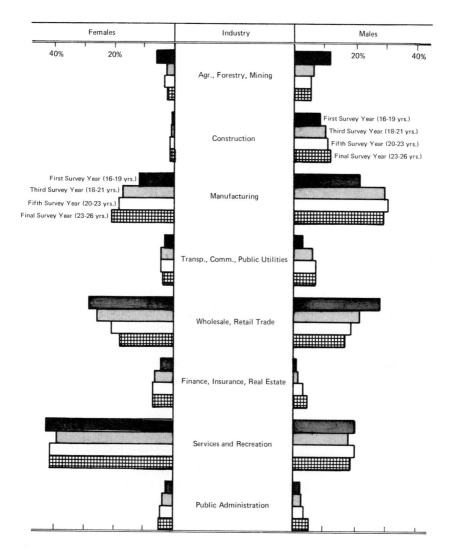

Source: National Longitudinal Surveys of Young Men and Young Women.

earlier cross section findings. (More detailed information is given in the four tables included in an appendix to this chapter, showing that blacks are less likely than whites to begin in professional or skilled occupations.)

By the time these cohorts of young men and women have reached the ages of 23 to 26, the employment patterns reflect fairly consistently those observed among adult workers. There will continue to be some movement out of unskilled or semiskilled jobs into the professions and other positions of greater responsibility, but as a group, adult work patterns are becoming well defined. It is at this point that the transition into primary jobs is under way. The characteristics of these jobs are well known. They tend to be stable and well paid, with opportunities for future growth and advancement.

In a comprehensive study of the occupational mobility of NLS young men, Andrew Kohen found that although considerable randomness is present in both the probability and quality of the occupational move, there are some identifiable trends.[1] Young blacks, for instance, are unlikely to enter managerial positions initially, and are even less likely to move into such positions as time passes. Furthermore, while the proportion of semiskilled operative workers declines among whites over time, it increases for young blacks. Mobility rates also vary significantly with occupation of initial post-school job. Professional and technical workers are among the least mobile, and unskilled workers are the most likely to move.

Kohen also demonstrated that young men are nearly twice as likely to advance occupationally if they no longer work for their first employer, reinforcing the idea that youths mill around in the labor market prior to settling down in a more permanent position. Moreover, for those changing employers, education and formal training are strongly related to occupational upgrading, while for those moving internally within a firm, ability, occupational information, and the lack of any health limitations have more pronounced effects.[2]

98

Wages, Weeks Worked, and Annual Earnings

It seems clear that, as a group, young workers move in a fairly predictable pattern through the job hierarchy. Comparing entry-level jobs held by young men in 1966 and the positions they held in 1971 reveals that only 40 percent were still employed in the same occupations. However, the changing employment patterns do not tell the whole story of labor market assimilation. The period of school-to-work transition also involves a change in the certainty, stability, and remuneration of employment. Figure 6-3 shows how the aging process is associated with increased hourly rates of pay, weeks of employment, and annual earnings. The wages earned by most teenagers are rather low. While the hourly earnings of males tend to be somewhat higher than those of females, the racial differences are relatively small. Within four years, the mean earnings of all groups have increased about 75 percent. Leading the gainers are white males whose earnings nearly double. These earnings are unadjusted for price changes, however.

Matching the gains in hourly earnings is the extent of employment as reflected by the number of weeks worked in the past 12 months. As teenagers, the women average less than 20 weeks of employment, with black women working fewer than 15 weeks per year. Males in their teens average more than 25 weeks of employment over the year. The annual work effort increases with age for all groups. By the time these individuals reach their mid-twenties, the women average more than 30 weeks per year and the men nearly 45 weeks. Racial differences become imperceptible. (Unfortunately, the information on the number of weeks unemployed is unreliable, making it difficult to ascertain the full extent of labor force participation over the year. There is some indication, however, that young blacks tend to spend more weeks in the labor force, with the difference showing up in the mean number of weeks unemployed.)

It appears that the occupational shifts observed earlier are associated with movements toward higher wages and greater stability, with longer periods of employment. This is also reflected in the higher labor force participation and lower unemployment observed earlier. Missing is the relationship of these measures to one another.

The best measure of the year's over-all labor market activity is annual wage and salary income. Labor earnings measured in this way reflect differences in hourly earnings, along with hours and weeks worked. They also account for periods out of the labor force and spells of unemployment. Furthermore, they serve not only as an indicator of the economic rewards to labor market activity, but are closely related to occupational status and peer group recognition. Among the individuals analyzed here, earnings in the first survey year are correlated as follows with weeks worked, weeks unemployed, weeks in the labor force, and the Duncan Index of Socioeconomic Status, respectively: 0.44; -0.26; 0.35; and 0.31.

Parts *e* and *f* of Figure 6-3 show the growth in earnings for whites and blacks, young men and young women, over the seven years covered by the NLS study. While there are discernible differences, all teenagers start at a fairly low level. Part-time work at low pay, interspersed with frequent periods out of the labor force or unemployed, does not generate large earnings. There are marked changes with aging. The behavior and employment patterns observed among the females result in a rather slow growth in earnings. Wage and salary income grows much more rapidly for males, with whites enjoying the greatest advance. The earnings of white males between the ages of 23 to 26 exceed those of blacks the same age by 30 percent. The ratio, when compared to the women, is nearly two to one. This is true even though the young women reach 23 to 26 years of age two years later than the young men (due to the two year difference in survey years), and as a result show some gains attributable to inflation.

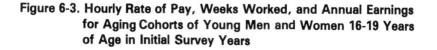

Figure 6-3. Hourly Rate of Pay, Weeks Worked, and Annual Earnings for Aging Cohorts of Young Men and Women 16-19 Years of Age in Initial Survey Years

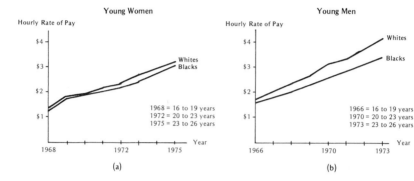

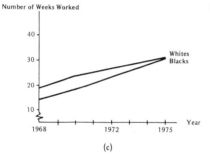

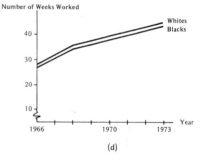

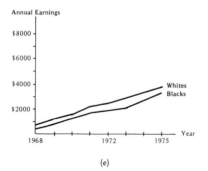

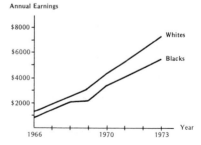

Source: National Longitudinal Surveys.

101

Early Labor Market Experience
and Future Employability

Although it is interesting to compare patterns for different groups, there is little surprise in finding that earnings grow as individuals move from their teens into adulthood. Of importance is the extent to which unsatisfactory experiences at an early age are related to subsequent labor market activity and success. Periods spent unemployed or out of the labor force deprive young and old alike of experience, contacts, and training. For the young, this loss of valuable work experience results in relative disadvantage later on.

School activities provide some valuable experience. Those unemployed or out of the labor force may be denied useful labor market experiences, but if they are still enrolled in school, the consequences are less likely to be harmful. Periods spent both out of school and out of work, however, could potentially be very harmful. Thus, in trying to relate past labor market activity to subsequent success, one must take into account the interaction between labor force participation and school enrollment.

Using the National Longitudinal Surveys, it is possible to compare early labor market experience with later measures of success. Even with extensive longitudinal data, it is difficult to construct comprehensive histories of individuals for comparison. It is possible, however, to compare labor force and school enrollment status in the initial survey year (when the aging cohorts are teenagers) as well as four years later (when they are young adults) to the final survey year labor market status. While this does not concentrate on or isolate those with chronic problems of youth unemployment, it does have the advantage of including those experiencing short-run transitional problems. This provides additional insight into the meaning and severity of the high youth unemployment figures.

Table 6-1 shows the relationship between labor force status in the final survey year and that experienced during earlier periods. While 92.4 percent of the young men and 60.0 percent of the young women were in the labor force in the final survey year, the proportions change considerably depending on earlier experiences. Those out of school and out of work as teenagers are far less likely to be current labor force participants. For those currently in the labor force, the probability of being unemployed is much higher if the teenage period was spent both out of work and out of school. Current labor force participation is highest for those who were employed as teenagers. As can be expected, being out of work but in school is not as closely related to subsequent employability as being out of work and out of school. Only for the women is teenage unemployment while in school related to later participation rates. Being out of the labor force while in school, however, has a negligible effect. Young adult labor force status is even more closely correlated with later experiences. Labor force participation is considerably lower and the probability of being unemployed in the final survey year is higher for both young men and young women who were out of school and out of work as young adults 20 to 23 years of age.

Early school enrollment and labor force status are clearly correlated with later labor market activity. Table 6-2 shows that this carries over to differences in wage and salary income. As discussed earlier, a variety of factors contribute to earning differences by race and sex. The important element, however, is that these differences are correlated with prior labor market activity. Once again, youths out of school and out of work as teenagers or young adults carry this disadvantage with them into the early adult years. The most serious disadvantage is found among those who spent an earlier period out of school and out of the labor force. Current earnings for these individuals are about half the average for their race-sex cohort.

There appears to be little question that, on the average, those having difficult labor market experiences as youths are the same individuals who have difficulties later on. While many unemployed youths successfully move into well-paying, permanent positions, many will not do so by the time they are in their mid-twenties and, as a result, face a real disadvantage as adult workers. Youths who are unemployed or out of the labor force,

Table 6-1. Labor Force Status in Final Survey Year by Earlier School Enrollment and Labor Force Status (percent distribution)

Status and age per survey year	Final survey year (23 to 26 years of age)					
	Men			Women		
	Employed	Unemployed	Out of labor force	Employed	Unemployed	Out of labor force
First survey year (16 to 19 years of age):						
In school						
Employed	92.2	5.1	2.7	67.8	8.4	23.8
Unemployed	92.0	8.0	0.0	51.4	6.8	41.9
Out of labor force	91.4	3.7	4.9	67.4	7.2	25.4
Out of school						
Employed	95.2	1.7	3.1	60.4	6.1	33.6
Unemployed	89.7	6.9	3.4	42.3	8.5	49.3
Out of labor force	78.9	7.9	13.2	37.7	7.7	54.5
Fifth survey year (20 to 23 years of age):						
In school						
Employed	95.4	3.3	1.3	91.7	1.7	6.6
Unemployed	100.0	0.0	0.0	57.1	14.3	28.6
Out of labor force	94.3	3.4	2.3	76.9	9.6	13.5

104

Out of school						
Employed	95.2	2.9	1.9	72.2	6.7	21.1
Unemployed	80.0	9.3	10.7	49.5	13.8	36.7
Out of labor force	62.2	13.3	24.4	32.8	7.5	59.7
Total	92.4	4.0	3.5	60.0	7.3	32.7
Size of sample	1,355	59	52	926	113	504

Source: National Longitudinal Surveys.

Table 6-2. Mean Earnings by Prior Labor Force and School Enrollment Status for Aging Cohorts of Young Men and Young Women Who Were Out of School in Final Survey Year

	Final survey year (23 to 26 years of age)			
	Men		Women	
Status and age per survey year	White	Black	White	Black
Size of sample	1,243	402	1,053	458
Grand mean	$7,308	$5,634	$3,646	$3,469
First survey year (16 to 19 years of age):				
In school				
Employed	$7,784	$5,797	$4,188	$4,295
Unemployed	6,858	5,644	3,465	3,224
Out of labor force	6,939	5,564	4,292	3,803
Out of school				
Employed	7,423	5,937	3,308	3,791
Unemployed	6,816	4,077	2,226	3,120
Out of labor force	4,676	3,921	1,962	1,879
	F = 3.25***	F = 1.60	F = 10.81****	F = 5.21****

Fifth survey year
(20 to 23 years of age):

In school				
Employed	$7,988	$6,036	$5,695	$5,985
Unemployed	8,036	4,550	5,344	4,118
Out of labor force	6,309	3,785	4,710	4,806
Out of school				
Employed	7,918	6,065	4,744	4,757
Unemployed	6,289	5,124	2,753	2,670
Out of labor force	3,959	2,084	1,222	1,530
	$F = 7.55$****	$F = 5.14$****	$F = 51.09$****	$F = 27.61$****

Source: National Longitudinal Surveys.

Significance levels: 10% (*) 5% (**) 1% (***) 0.1% (****).

and are also out of school, define an important target population that can be expected to find labor force assimilation difficult. This is especially true if they are blacks or women.

The Net Effect of Youth Labor Force Status

Youth labor force status, in conjunction with school enrollment, provides an early warning indicator of those most likely to incur problems in making the school-to-work transition. What is not clear is whether youth joblessness itself contributes to later difficulties. It may be that the same factors contributing to early labor market experiences are operating later on as well. Whether or not differences remain after one controls for socioeconomic background, education, and other personal traits is not clear.

Table 6-3 shows the results of multiple regression analysis designed to isolate factors which explain differences in earnings of young adults who are out of school. The groups analyzed consist of young men and young women who were 16 to 19 years of age in the initial survey year and out of school in the final survey year. Earnings are observed seven years after the initial survey when the group ranges in age from 23 to 26. Each cohort is partitioned on the basis of race, the effect of which on earnings has already been established.

Stratified by race and sex, the regression equations explain between 13 and 29 percent of the variation in annual wage and salary income. Age, education, and marital status have significant effects upon earnings. Earnings tend to rise with age, even within the small range represented here, and also to increase with each year of school completed. This is true for blacks as well as for whites. Furthermore, the returns to additional schooling for blacks, as measured in the early 1970s, do not differ substantially from those for whites. This extremely important finding supports the evidence of increasing returns to education for young blacks in the 1970s.

Socioeconomic status does not appear to have its expected effect upon earnings after one controls for education,[3] although labor market knowledge, which is highly correlated with background, is directly related to earnings and may result from some influences of family environment. Labor market knowledge also serves as a proxy for general intelligence as measured by IQ scores. For younger men, being married is associated with nearly $2,000 per year in additional earnings. Women, on the other hand, earn less if they are married. Men living in a city or its suburbs can expect to earn more than comparable rural residents (these statistics are not available for women).

An additional variable is included: in each survey year, respondents were asked if any training was received in addition to formal schooling, and if the training was ever used on the job. With this information it is possible to isolate the individuals who received and used training during the school-to-work transition. One out of three respondents indicated that he or she had received and used such training. Blacks were less likely than whites to participate in training, and young men less likely than young women.

The differences in earnings associated with training used on the job are substantial, ranging from about $1,500 per year for whites to more than $2,300 for black women. Along with the data on years of school completed, this finding for out-of-school youth is highly significant in policy terms for those concerned with the low earnings of youth and the differences by race and sex. Although these results do not distinguish among specific training programs, they do indicate that when training is tailored to the needs of the labor market as well as the individual, reflected in use on the job, the gains are generally substantial and lasting. More important, these gains are present for young men and young women, black and white, and appear to be higher for blacks.

Controlling for these correlates of wage and salary earnings, one can also determine how the early labor market experiences of youth affect subsequent earnings. At issue is whether individuals with roughly equivalent backgrounds but different early labor market experiences can expect subsequent earnings to differ in a predictable manner. Table 6-4 allows such comparisons after

109

Table 6-3. Correlates of Variations in Wage and Salary Income in Final Survey Year for Out-of-School Young Men and Young Women[a]

Explanatory variables	Males		Females	
	White	Black	White	Black
Age	338.80 (2.78)***	235.46 (1.41)*	-95.99 (0.94)	296.00 (2.29)**
Years of school completed	227.67 (3.41)****	170.24 (1.85)**	357.62 (6.47)	404.69 (5.64)****
Socioeconomic status	4.17 (0.54)	18.12 (1.60)*	-1.33 (0.20)	9.36 (1.20)
Married	1,909.44 (6.86)****	1,987.58 (5.43)****	-1,846.89 (7.37)****	-431.93 (1.49)*
Living in SMSA	959.97 (3.59)****	678.10 (1.59)*	n.a.	n.a.
Labor market knowledge	44.90 (2.08)**	10.82 (0.38)	250.15 (3.48)****	207.82 (3.05)***
Training[b]	1,546.50 (5.33)****	1,933.76 (4.12)****	1,569.69 (6.44)****	2,339.04 (6.72)****

110

R² (adjusted)	0.13	0.19	0.18	0.29
Degrees of freedom	1,008	299	980	384
Standard error	4,087	3,154	3,490	2,788
F- value	22.77	11.44	36.37	26.61

Source: National Longitudinal Surveys.

Significance levels: 10% (*) 5% (**) 1% (***) 0.1% (****).

[a]Wage and salary income reported in final survey year for those who were 16-19 years of age in initial survey year.

[b]Dichotomous variable assuming value 1 for those who received training and reported using it on the job and zero otherwise.

Table 6-4. Adjusted Mean Earnings by Prior Labor Force and School Enrollment Status for Aging Cohorts of Young Men and Young Women Who Were Out of School in Final Survey Year

Status and age per survey year	Final survey year (23 to 26 years of age)			
	Men		Women	
	White	Black	White	Black
Size of sample	1,015	307	987	391
Grand mean	$7,650	$5,740	$3,752	$3,584
First survey year (16 to 19 years of age):				
In school				
Employed	$7,920	$5,971	$3,798	$3,882
Unemployed	7,433	6,139	3,171	2,881
Out of labor force	7,651	6,188	4,040	3,756
Out of school				
Employed	7,476	5,560	3,772	3,912
Unemployed	7,037	4,422	3,292	2,961
Out of labor force	6,140	3,854	3,079	2,924
	F = 1.74	F = 2.57**	F = 8.26****	F = 3.99***

Fifth survey year
(20 to 23 years of age):

In school				
Employed	$8,135	$4,818	$4,708	$4,711
Unemployed	7,752	3,605	4,761	4,320
Out of labor force	7,323	4,028	4,072	4,099
Out of school				
Employed	8,082	6,185	4,704	4,530
Unemployed	6,980	4,916	2,615	3,091
Out of labor force	5,508	3,608	1,998	2,157
	F = 5.84****	F = 4.32****	F = 42.48****	F = 21.06****

Source: National Longitudinal Surveys.

Significance levels: 10% (*) 5% (**) 1% (***) 0.1% (****).

[a]Adjusted to account for differences in age, education, training, socioeconomic status, labor market knowledge, marital status, and (for males) living in a SMSA.

adjusting for differences in the variables included in Table 6-3. The observations are stratified by race and sex to account for these differences.

The results are based on Multiple Classification Analysis, a technique which combines linear regression estimates and analysis of variance to test for significant differences in mean values of a dependent variable after controlling for the effects of other variables included in the model. The procedure involves computing the regression equation which allows estimation of mean earnings for an individual with average measures on all the variables controlled for. This is done for each of the separate groups (in this case for each school enrollment and labor force status category). Sums of squares are then estimated and used to compute an F- statistic which tests for significant differences among the adjusted means.

The differences in the adjusted means are not as pronounced as the differences for unadjusted means reported in Table 6-2, but the same general patterns emerge. Again, being without a job while out of school seems to have an adverse effect on subsequent earnings. The impact is more pronounced when the experience occurs between the ages of 20 and 24, but teenage labor force status is also related to subsequent wage and salary earnings.

Whether for young men or young women, black or white, time spent out of school and out of the labor force represents a loss of experience that is associated with a clear earnings disadvantage later on. While the effect is not so great, being unemployed during the school-to-work transition also has an adverse effect. This is particularly true if the spell of unemployment comes while the person is out of school. Those who experience unemployment while in school can expect to earn less on an average than those successfully employed while in school or out of the labor force and devoting full time to school activities.

The differences by race and sex are also pronounced. Among young men, out-of-school black youth are more seriously affected by adverse early labor market experiences. Among young women, however, no differences by race are apparent. Young women,

114

black and white, however, are more seriously affected by adverse early labor market experiences than young men.

The findings presented here contradict the thesis that unemployment is a phase through which every youth passes with no long term adverse consequences. Clearly, it is never possible to control for all differences in personal characteristics, background, and experience. Nonetheless, the fact that early labor market status continues to be related to subsequent earnings after adjusting for those factors which are consistently found related to labor market experiences does provide some strong evidence of long term effects.

Indeed, the most significant finding here is that youth labor market status is not only related to, but seems to have an effect of its own on, subsequent employability and income. Marketable skills can be learned on the job or in school, but periods spent out of school and either voluntarily or involuntarily without work, represent a loss that is likely to be felt for years. This supports the conclusion that labor market policies aimed at providing employment for out-of-school youth who are out of work will pay off both immediately and for years to come. The sizable returns to training received outside formal schooling during the period of labor market assimilation are also important in this context, along with the returns to formal education.

Policies aimed at creating youth jobs while providing useful and productive skills have a double impact on the subsequent employability and general labor market success of youth.

NOTES

1. Andrew Kohen, "Antecedents and Consequences of Occupational Mobility," *Career Thresholds,* 6, U.S. Department of Labor, Employment and Training Administration (1977).

2. Similar trends are reported in Michael Ornstein, *Entry into the American Labor Force* (New York: Academic Press, 1976); and Marcia Freedman, "The Youth Labor Market," in *From School to Work: Improving the Transition,* National Commission for Manpower Policy (Washington, D.C.: U.S. Government Printing Office, 1976).

3. Herbert Parnes and Andrew Kohen, "Labor Market Experience of Noncollege Youth," in *From School to Work: Improving the Transition.* National Commission for Manpower Policy (Washington, D.C.: U.S. Government Printing Office, 1976). Parnes and Kohen show, however, that measures of occupational mobility are related to socioeconomic status among young men.

APPENDIX

The following tables are included to provide more detailed information than the tables and charts presented in the last two chapters. Differences due to race and sex are more explicit and some additional labor market experience information is included.

Appendix Table 6-1. Employment by Occupation of Current or Last Job by Survey Year for Young Men Who Were 16 to 19 Years of Age in 1966 (percent distribution)

Occupation	Whites				Blacks			
	1966	1968	1970	1973	1966	1968	1970	1973
Professional, technical and kindred	4.5	10.1	14.6	18.4	1.4	4.5	9.7	9.2
Managers, officers and proprietors	1.0	3.3	6.5	11.9	0.3	0.9	2.4	3.9
Clerical and kindred	9.7	12.0	10.3	9.6	7.7	12.3	12.6	8.3
Sales workers	6.1	4.9	7.1	6.6	2.6	0.9	3.1	2.4
Craftsmen, foremen, and kindred	10.2	11.2	17.2	20.4	5.6	7.6	10.2	15.1
Operators and kindred	23.2	27.3	23.9	18.2	23.9	33.1	29.8	36.5
Private household workers	0.3	0.0	0.0	0.0	0.0	0.0	0.0	0.0
Service workers except private household	14.8	9.2	6.3	4.5	20.9	14.1	10.4	8.3
Farmers and farm managers	0.3	0.8	1.6	2.1	0.2	0.0	0.2	0.0
Farm laborers and foremen	9.0	3.7	2.3	1.3	13.7	5.4	3.6	2.2
Laborers except farm and mine	21.0	17.5	10.3	7.1	23.8	21.2	17.9	14.1
Total number	1,436	1,124	1,096	1,260	585	462	413	411

Source: National Longitudinal Surveys.

Appendix Table 6-2. Employment by Industry of Current or Last Job by Survey Year for Young Men Who Were 16 to 19 Years of Age in 1966 (percent distribution)

Industry	Whites				Blacks			
	1966	1968	1970	1973	1966	1968	1970	1973
Agriculture, forestry, and fisheries	10.6	5.9	4.6	4.2	16.0	6.3	5.1	2.7
Mining	0.3	0.6	0.6	0.9	0.0	0.0	0.2	0.7
Construction	8.8	11.4	11.8	12.9	8.8	8.5	8.0	9.8
Manufacturing	22.2	28.2	29.7	28.3	20.2	35.7	35.4	36.3
Transportation, communication, and public utilities	2.8	6.7	7.0	6.3	4.6	5.7	6.8	11.3
Wholesale/retail trade	32.2	24.4	20.1	17.9	21.8	19.2	16.0	16.2
Finance, insurance, and real estate	1.9	2.1	3.8	4.8	1.0	1.7	1.9	2.5
Services and recreation	19.3	17.5	19.3	19.7	22.5	20.2	23.5	16.7
Public administration	2.0	3.1.	3.2	5.0	4.9	2.6	2.9	3.9
Total number	1,440	1,121	1,092	1,260	588	459	412	408

Source: National Longitudinal Surveys.

Appendix Table 6-3. Employment by Occupation of Current or Last Job by Survey Year for Young Women Who Were 16 to 19 Years of Age in 1968 (percent distribution)

Occupation	Whites				Blacks			
	1968	1970	1972	1975	1968	1970	1972	1975
Professional and kindred	2.9	6.3	13.8	21.8	3.5	2.9	8.0	13.3
Managers, officers, and proprietors	0.5	1.0	1.8	3.3	0.0	0.4	0.6	1.4
Clerical and kindred	34.5	44.1	43.3	37.5	28.6	41.5	35.1	29.9
Sales workers	11.9	8.7	6.8	6.8	3.9	4.7	5.4	3.6
Craftsmen, foremen, and kindred	0.3	0.6	0.6	1.0	0.0	0.4	0.4	0.8
Operatives and kindred	10.0	11.4	12.5	10.9	11.8	14.1	17.8	23.6
Private household workers	15.1	6.0	3.7	2.5	16.9	10.2	7.4	3.6
Other service workers	21.8	20.1	16.1	14.7	21.7	21.1	21.0	19.8
Farmers and farm managers	0.0	0.0	0.1	0.3	0.0	0.0	0.0	0.0
Farm laborers and foremen	2.5	1.1	1.0	0.6	13.2	4.5	3.2	1.8
Laborers except farm and mine	0.6	0.7	0.2	0.6	0.5	0.2	1.1	2.0
Total number	1,029	1,211	1,228	1,156	433	511	538	495

Source: National Longitudinal Surveys.

Appendix Table 6-4. Employment by Industry of Current or Last Job by Survey Year for Young Women Who Were 16 to 19 Years of Age in 1968 (percent distribution)

Industry	Whites				Blacks			
	1968	1970	1972	1975	1968	1970	1972	1975
Agriculture, forestry, and fisheries	3.0	1.5	1.5	1.6	13.5	4.5	3.4	2.0
Mining	0.1	0.0	0.2	0.3	0.0	0.0	0.0	0.0
Construction	0.4	0.4	0.6	0.9	0.0	0.0	0.2	0.2
Manufacturing	13.5	17.9	18.6	19.3	7.7	15.7	18.1	25.8
Transportation, communication, and public utilities	3.5	4.4	4.6	3.7	3.9	5.3	4.5	4.5
Wholesale/retail trade	32.7	28.6	22.4	20.3	16.5	18.3	18.1	14.7
Finance, insurance, and real estate	4.8	6.6	8.0	7.3	2.6	6.7	6.0	6.1
Services and recreation	39.8	37.1	40.3	41.5	52.0	43.7	43.7	40.9
Public administration	2.3	3.3	3.9	5.3	3.9	5.7	5.8	5.7
Total number	1,031	1,205	1,217	1,148	431	508	530	489

Source: National Longitudinal Surveys.

Appendix Table 6-5. Labor Market Experience for Aging Cohort of Males Who Were 16-19 in 1966, by Survey Year, Age, and Race

Characteristics of the labor market experience	1966 (16-19) White	1966 (16-19) Black	1968 (18-21) White	1968 (18-21) Black	1969 (19-22) White	1969 (19-22) Black	1970 (20-23) White	1970 (20-23) Black	1971 (21-24) White	1971 (21-24) Black	1973 (23-26) White	1973 (23-26) Black
Survey week												
Percent in school	71.8	62.2	49.0	33.7	39.6	21.2	28.8	16.2	22.3	11.5	14.7	10.1
Percent in labor force	67.0	71.1	74.4	81.4	81.1	85.1	85.8	89.4	91.5	92.0	92.3	94.1
Percent employed	88.6	81.5	94.2	91.7	94.3	90.0	92.7	88.2	93.2	88.5	97.0	93.2
Percent part time	48.0	35.6	27.0	17.6	n.a.	n.a.	13.4	10.5	n.a.	n.a.	n.a.	n.a.
Percent full time	40.6	45.9	67.2	74.1	n.a.	n.a.	79.3	77.7	n.a.	n.a.	n.a.	n.a.
Hours worked	27.8	29.2	37.0	36.3	37.9	38.3	39.8	38.5	41.7	39.8	n.a.	n.a.
Percent unemployed	11.4	18.5	5.8	8.3	5.7	10.0	7.3	11.8	6.9	11.5	3.0	6.8
Percent out of labor force	33.0	28.9	25.6	18.6	18.9	14.9	14.2	10.6	8.5	8.0	7.7	5.9
Current or last job												
Wages per hour (dollars)	1.63	1.55	2.32	2.02	2.71	2.34	3.10	2.55	3.35	2.81	n.a.	n.a.
Duncan Index	21.8	16.3	28.3	20.8	31.3	23.6	34.3	25.3	36.2	24.7	40.4	26.6
Percent secondary jobs	50.7	55.7	29.9	36.5	24.1	32.8	n.a.	n.a.	n.a.	n.a.	n.a.	n.a.
Percent intermediate jobs	21.3	22.6	24.5	30.7	20.9	27.4	n.a.	n.a.	n.a.	n.a.	n.a.	n.a.
Past year												
Weeks worked	28.1	26.0	35.5	34.6	37.6	36.8	n.a.	n.a.	n.a.	n.a.	45.3	44.0
Weeks unemployed	1.9	2.9	1.3	2.9	1.6	3.2	2.2	3.9	3.3	5.4	5.0	8.1
Wage and salary income (dollars)	1,133.9	834.5	2,563.1	2,113.9	3,561.8	2,988.4	4,360.2	3,495.6	5,145.3	3,997.9	7,308.4	5,634.4

Source: National Longitudinal Surveys.

123

Appendix Table 6-6. Labor Market Experience for Aging Cohort of Females Who Were 16-19 in 1968, by Survey Year, Age, and Race

Characteristics of the labor market experience	1968 (16-19) White	1968 (16-19) Black	1969 (17-20) White	1969 (17-20) Black	1970 (18-21) White	1970 (18-21) Black	1971 (19-22) White	1971 (19-22) Black	1972 (20-23) White	1972 (20-23) Black	1973 (21-24) White	1973 (21-24) Black	1975 (23-26) White	1975 (23-26) Black
Survey week														
Percent in school	64.4	60.9	52.3	44.0	35.2	28.2	26.9	19.2	19.2	15.7	12.9	11.5	9.0	7.5
Percent in labor force	47.0	42.7	52.9	49.4	54.8	52.8	55.1	56.2	56.7	55.8	56.6	54.7	55.5	56.5
Percent employed	82.6	70.1	86.4	72.2	86.4	74.9	89.5	77.2	90.0	80.8	92.5	84.7	92.5	81.8
Percent part time	45.0	34.7	n.a.	n.a.	25.1	17.9	n.a.	n.a.	18.7	15.5	15.1	8.9	n.a.	n.a.
Percent full time	37.6	35.4	n.a.	n.a.	61.3	57.0	n.a.	n.a.	71.3	65.3	77.4	75.8	n.a.	n.a.
Hours worked	24.7	25.6	27.7	31.2	32.5	33.2	33.8	32.7	35.0	35.4	36.5	36.5	36.8	37.9
Percent unemployed	17.4	29.9	13.6	27.8	13.6	25.1	10.5	22.8	10.0	19.2	7.5	15.3	7.5	18.2
Percent out of labor force	53.0	57.3	47.1	50.6	45.2	47.2	44.9	43.8	43.3	44.2	43.4	45.3	44.5	43.5
Current or last job														
Wages per hour (dollars)	1.38	1.31	1.63	1.61	1.86	1.78	2.17	2.00	2.41	2.23	2.67	2.46	3.24	3.14
Duncan Index	30.6	24.5	n.a.	n.a.	36.3	30.9	38.3	31.4	39.9	32.1	41.4	33.4	43.4	34.1
Percent secondary jobs	n.a.	n.a.	n.a.	n.a.	n.a.	n.a.	n.a.	n.a.	n.a.	n.a.	n.a.	n.a.	n.a.	n.a.
Percent intermediate jobs	n.a.	n.a.	n.a.	n.a.	n.a.	n.a.	n.a.	n.a.	n.a.	n.a.	n.a.	n.a.	n.a.	n.a.
Past year														
Weeks worked	18.0	13.6	n.a.	n.a.	23.0	18.0	n.a.	n.a.	n.a.	n.a.	n.a.	n.a.	30.9	31.0
Weeks unemployed	6.2	7.9	5.8	7.7	5.8	6.6	6.6	8.7	5.5	9.2	5.6	9.5	n.a.	n.a.
Wage and salary income (dollars)	611.4	400.6	1,047.9	825.0	1,557.9	1,264.1	2,024.0	1,562.2	2,427.5	1,952.0	2,744.9	2,313.2	3,779.8	3,535.8

Source: National Longitudinal Surveys.

124

A Reassessment
of Youth Unemployment

By
Arvil V. Adams and Garth L. Mangum

Unemployment among 16 to 24 year olds reached record levels in the mid-1970s, accounting for nearly one of every two unemployed Americans. By comparison, 16 to 24 year olds accounted for one of every five of the employed. Youth unemployment, as a result, has moved to the forefront of public concern. But among the many concerns facing those involved in public policy today, ranging from the deterioration of urban centers to meeting the energy needs of tomorrow, what priority should be given to combating youth unemployment? Is it a problem that every youth faces in the career development process and passes through with no long term adverse consequences? Indeed, is there any real economic hardship in their short term joblessness, since many unemployed youth are enrolled in school and continue to live at home?

To some youths, for example, unemployment plays a functional role in the building of bridges between school and work. In this context, job search provides an inexpensive learning process helping youth adjust to the realities of the labor market and make career choices. Recent shifts in demographic patterns leading to a relative decline in the youth population, moreover, may contribute to the solution without requiring public intervention.

These are important issues to be considered in determining what priority America should assign to creating jobs for youths. Beyond is the determination of what policies, if any, are appropriate to the solution. To what extent is the problem responsive to macro policies of economic stimulation and to what extent are micro policies which focus on the problem's structural dimensions needed? This chapter reassesses the youth unemployment problem, its causes and consequences, and discusses the lessons for public policy derived from the study. While concerned with youth 16 to 24 years of age, special attention is focused on teenage unemployment.

An Overview

The study is based on analysis of recent trends in youth unemployment from published sources and on additional analysis of a national sample of young people 16 to 19 years of age who were followed longitudinally over a seven-year period in the late 1960s and early 1970s. Several important findings emerge from the analysis. Among the most significant for public policy are:

1. Unemployment of out-of-school youth does have a "hangover" effect. Those who have unfavorable early labor market experiences are less likely than others to have favorable subsequent experiences, education, and other background characteristics held constant.

2. Education and training have a significant positive effect upon the employment and earnings of youth, by race and sex.

3. Tight labor markets in the 1980s will reduce youth unemployment from its record levels in the mid-1970s, but will not eliminate it. A substantial structural difference between youth and adult unemployment will persist.

126

4. Demographic trends leading to a reduction in the youth population will reduce the visibility of youth unemployment in the 1980s, but not for blacks. Reductions in the black youth population will lag behind those for whites.

The last of the postwar baby boom will pass through their teenage years by 1981. The youth population will decline thereafter in relative and absolute terms through the 1980s. The teenage labor force, in turn, is expected to decline from its 1975 level of 8.8 million to 7.9 million in 1985. The decline will occur among black and white youths, but for blacks the decline will be more gradual as a consequence of their birth rates peaking later than those of whites and declining more slowly. In 1985, black teenagers are expected to account for slightly over 15 percent of the teenage labor force, increasing from 13 percent in 1975 and 11 percent in 1970. Based upon these patterns, youth unemployment will likely diminish in absolute terms in the 1980s, but its relative visibility among blacks will increase.

The postwar baby boom had an important impact upon youth unemployment in the 1960s and 1970s. The ratio of youth to adult unemployment nearly doubled in this period from its base of three to one during the 1950s and early 1960s. Many youth in the later period were unemployed simply because there were so many of them. The effect of this influx of young people, however, has already begun to dissipate and will largely disappear in the 1980s. By 1975, the ratio of youth to adult unemployment appeared to be returning to its historical base. With this happening, the high youth unemployment rates of today can be attributed, in major part, to the higher general levels of unemployment present in the economy. Since overall unemployment was at an historical high for an economic recovery period, youth unemployment as a multiple of the adult rate was certain to be extraordinarily high. However, even if this is reduced through economic stimulation, the structural relationship of youth to adult unemployment will remain as a serious problem.

The transition from school to work is marked by intermittent employment experiences. Teenage entry and reentry into the labor force, plus the part-time status of many youth jobs, combine to create a highly unstable employment pattern in comparison to the experience of adult workers. In 1976 nearly 70 percent of all unemployed teenagers were new entrants or reentrants to the labor force. Roughly 40 percent were never gainfully employed. Half of all unemployed workers were job losers, as compared with 23 percent for unemployed teenagers. Thus, much of the unemployment experienced by youths in contrast to adults can be attributed to the job search effort associated with turnover, interruptions in employment, and initial labor market entry.

One out of three unemployed 16 to 24 year olds is enrolled in school. Among teenagers, the number approaches one out of two. The nature of the youth employment experience differs substantially by school enrollment status. Whereas youths enrolled in school and unable to find work can withdraw from the search and focus on student activities, their out-of-school counterparts often have no such retreat and must continue to search. Youth unemployment rates among out-of-school youths exceed those of in-school youths by as much as two to one for 16 to 17 year olds.

The type of work sought also differs. Over half of all in-school youths 16 to 21 years of age in 1975 were looking for part-time jobs contrasted with only 6 percent among out-of-school youths. Whereas 15 percent of the in-school youths had voluntarily left their last job, less than half this number among out-of-school youths had done so. Among the employed, nine out of ten in-school teenagers held part-time jobs, compared with one out of ten out-of-school teenagers. These differences lead to consideration of work among in-school youths as a secondary activity and among out-of-school youths as a primary activity.

Other structural differences in youth unemployment are apparent by race. For two decades beginning in the mid-1950s, the ratio of black to white teenage unemployment has been rising from 1.3 in 1954 to 2.2 in 1976. Projections for the mid-1980s suggest that this trend will continue. Among the possible causes of this pattern is the postwar mass migration of southern blacks to northern cities where economic conditions have slowly, or in some cases rapidly, deteriorated. Jobs have fled the central city to the suburbs and nonmetropolitan areas. Clustered in central cities, black youths are confronted with low or even negative employment growth within key industrial and occupational categories which traditionally have been heavy employers of teenagers. This in turn has led to jobless rates for central city youths considerably above teenage unemployment rates in suburban and nonmetropolitan areas. These rates in metropolitan poverty areas reached 43 percent for black teenagers in 1976.

The analysis of longitudinal data adds further insight into the structural character of youth employment experiences during the transition from school to work. Differences in the labor market experience by race and sex begin during the teenage years. These differences are evident in the rate of pay, the amount of time at work, and the industry and occupation of employment. By the time teenagers have reached early adulthood, 23 to 26 years of age, white males have pulled well ahead of blacks and women in terms of their earnings. In contrast to earlier studies in the 1960s, this study indicates that the smoothness of the transition from school to work for young men and women, black and white, is related to the extent of education and training. Education in this case is measured by years of school completed and training represents training used on the job and acquired outside formal schooling. The results point very clearly to the positive effects of education and training upon the employment and earnings of youths by race and sex.

Perhaps the most important finding in terms of assigning priority to youth employment policies is that early labor market experiences of out-of-school teenagers are related to subsequent measures of labor market success after controlling for education and other background characteristics. This relationship is most pronounced among blacks and women, but does not apply to in-school teenage youth.

This finding, of course, should be qualified, given that one can never fully control for the pre-labor market experiences and

129

characteristics that influence both early and subsequent labor market experience. Nevertheless, the finding that foregone labor market experience during youth is associated with a reduction in subsequent earnings is fully supported by economic theory. The qualification, therefore, is most likely a matter of degree.

Based upon the longitudinal data, this finding sharply contradicts the thesis that teenage unemployment is a transitory problem experienced by most, but with no long term adverse consequences. With work the primary activity of out-of-school youths, joblessness can be expected to lead to loss of experience, information, and skills, hindering their successful assimilation into the labor force.

Lessons for Youth Employment Policy

With few exceptions, youth employment policies throughout the 1960s and early 1970s focused upon basic education, classroom and on-the-job training, and work experience. More recently, with passage of the Youth Employment and Demonstration Projects Act in 1977, attention has turned to public service employment and job creation. The creation of youth jobs in the public and private sector is an important step in responding to the youth unemployment challenge, but it should take place alongside other labor market policies in efforts to achieve a comprehensive solution to the problem. No single policy is likely to respond to the needs of such a diverse population. The results of this study offer several important lessons for youth employment policy.

General Labor Market Policies

The results of this study identify the need for general labor market policies which are not directly concerned with youths but which, nevertheless, would have an important impact upon youth employment opportunities. Such policies involve full employment, urban development, immigration, and social security. Youth unemployment today is no higher relative to adult unemployment than it was prior to the influx of youths into the labor force during the early 1960s. As such, the record levels of youth unemployment present today are due in large part to high general unemployment rates. Labor force and employment projections for 1985 indicate that reducing overall unemployment to 4.8 percent would reduce unemployment among 16 to 24 year olds to 12.6 percent. While reducing youth unemployment from its 1976 level of around 15 percent, however, overall economic stimulation would not solve the basic structural problems underlying differences in youth and adult unemployment rates.

One out of three unemployed teenagers are clustered in the nation's central cities. America's central cities are themselves fighting for economic survival. For them to survive there must be new emphasis given to urban development, and with this must come policies concerned with the blight and destitution of the ghetto, its crowded schools and low-income housing, its drug culture and crime. Together, these conditions serve to perpetuate economic and social inequality among those who must endure them. Accordingly, concern for youth unemployment must be joined with the broader challenge raised by urban development and the survival of the nation's central cities. In addition to programs of urban development, there should be policies offering assistance to those within central cities who are willing to relocate where jobs can be found.

In both urban and rural areas, youth must compete with others for dwindling numbers of low-skill jobs. Such competition must be accepted in a market economy, except where it comes from illegal sources. In this context, the continued influx of undocumented workers exacerbates youth labor market problems. Those who are willing to work "hard and scared" in low-skill jobs for low wages compete with youths for jobs. No one knows for certain the number of undocumented aliens, but estimates vary from 6 to 12 million with the number continuing to grow. Doubtless many of these persons compete for the 20 million or more youth jobs available today. There is, accordingly, an urgent need for public policy concerned with reducing the flow of undocumented workers.

131

Though not representing a source of illegal competition for youth jobs, the impact of older workers upon youth employment should be of concern to policymakers. Congress has agreed to double to $6,000 by 1982 the ceiling on earnings allowed without loss of social security benefits. This will further increase the competition for part-time jobs, a major source of youth employment. A difficult policy issue is involved, and one which requires recognition of its full distributional effects. It is doubtful, on the other hand, that raising the mandatory age of retirement would have any adverse effect upon youth employment, as youths are not likely to compete for jobs vacated through retirement. To the extent that older workers would delay beginning a "second career" or seeking part-time employment, raising the retirement age may actually reduce competition for some youth jobs.

Youth Labor Market Policies

"A rising tide raises all boats," but if the differential between youth and adult unemployment is to be reduced, special youth policies will be required.

Job Creation. Macro policies of economic stimulation and job creation are an important, if not essential, step to be taken in response to the youth employment dilemma. As suggested earlier, however, these policies do not address the basic structural dimensions of the problem. Moreover, such policies are not an efficient means of targeting job creation and can lead to unnecessary inflationary pressures. What is needed is a program of youth job creation that delivers jobs where needed most. Jobs are needed most by out-of-school youth because of the primary role of work within this population and the long term adverse effects of being out of school without a job. In 1976 an average of 6.4 million youths 16 to 24 years of age were out of school and unemployed or out of the labor force; this is a target group for job creation efforts.

Not all of the 6.4 million would have accepted jobs if offered, however. Over 4.0 million of them were out of the labor force. Of these, about 3 percent or 120 thousand had given up looking for work because they thought jobs were unavailable. When these discouraged youths are added to the number of unemployed youths, it yields a total of 2.5 million youths 16 to 24 years of age who want work but who cannot find it. This figure would doubtless be larger if jobs were guaranteed. Some youths who are out of the labor force and not aware of wanting a job under current conditions would change their status to that of looking for work if jobs were available. No estimate of this number is possible, however.

Some frictional unemployment is inevitable in the functioning of a dynamic labor market, as workers and firms search for the best match. It is doubtful that youth unemployment can ever be reduced to the same frictional level as that of adults, given differences in the employment experience of the two. Instead, if youth unemployment were reduced to as low as 8.5 percent, a rate achieved during the 1960s, representing a 40 percent drop from the 1976 rate of just under 15 percent, this would produce a frictional level of 1.3 million unemployed out-of-school youths. Achieving this goal would require 1.2 million jobs.

This need for 1.2 million jobs would be reduced further if the decision were made not to create jobs for out-of-school 16 and 17 year olds which might encourage youths to drop out of school. If only half the number of jobs needed for this age group were created and tied to retention in school, the total number of youth jobs needed would fall to 1.1 million.

Some of the 1.1 million jobs needed to reduce out-of-school youth unemployment to 8.5 percent would be created through macro policies of economic stimulation. Based on earlier projections, assuming a total unemployment rate just under 5 percent, over 300 thousand additional jobs would be attained by youths. The remaining 800 thousand jobs would require direct job creation programs. This figure represents a conservative estimate, since it does not attempt to account for the labor supply effect of a guaranteed jobs program on out-of-school youth who are currently out of the labor force.

To put in proper perspective the 800 thousand jobs needed to reduce out-of-school youth unemployment to 8.5 percent, it might be useful to observe that this number surpasses the 1978 target of 725 thousand public service employment jobs under the Comprehensive Employment and Training Act. It seems clear that if a substantive effort is to be made in response to the critical need for youth jobs, it will require a partnership between the public and private sectors. It is hardly feasible, in terms of spending constraints, or necessarily desirable, to create this number of jobs in the public sector. The comparative advantages of both sectors should be exploited instead.

Job creation in the public sector has the advantage of being an active rather than a passive policy response. It does not depend upon the consumption and investment decisions of households and firms to create jobs. Instead, these jobs can be created quickly and targeted to specific populations as needed through public service employment. The number of jobs needed, however, as well as reliance upon a market economy, indicates that other job creation efforts will be required within the private sector. The challenge here will be to target job creation efforts properly so that, in reaching the desired population, expenditures will not produce unnecessary pressures on price stability. With this in mind, it could be argued that public sector job creation efforts for youths should be directed to where the jobs are most difficult to create, that is, where the private sector response will be most difficult to stimulate.

This strategy would require a thorough knowledge of the job creation capacity of the private sector under alternative program incentive structures. One might expect, however, that jobs in the private sector would be easiest to create within nonmetropolitan areas where they are already increasing, excluding some rural areas, and most difficult to create in metropolitan areas, particularly within central cities. Based upon characteristics of youths, jobs in the private sector may be more difficult to create for younger rather than older members of the youth cohort. If, for example, public service employment were focused on out-of-school youths without jobs in central cities who were 18 to 19 years old, the number of public sector jobs required would fall to approximately 60 thousand.

The jobs program described here would exploit the comparative advantage of public sector job creation. In addition to reaching those for whom jobs are most difficult to create, standby job creation capacity would be needed to guarantee jobs to those not reached by the private sector. The number here would depend upon the incentive structure for youth job creation offered to the private sector and the success of macro policies in economic stimulation. Incentives to the private sector for youth job creation could include wage subsidies, tax credits, and even moral suasion. Numerous proposals of this nature are available and the Carter Administration has proposed spending $400 million in such efforts in fiscal 1979. In targeting these programs, however, attention should be given to minimizing the substitution of youths for adult workers and the subsidization of employers without creating new jobs. Tradeoffs of this kind may occasionally be necessary, and can be justified in some cases based upon the economic returns to work experience among out-of-school youths and the length of time over which these returns will be realized by the individual and society. This is not to discount the importance of equity considerations, however.

Much has been said concerning the number of jobs to be created and ways in which this could be accomplished, while little has been said about the type of jobs to be offered. Some would consider it desirable, for example, if all youth jobs were "meaningful." Yet, this may be the opposite of what should be offered to 16 and 17 year olds. If the jobs are too attractive, this may encourage them to drop out of school. As this study has shown, school retention is an important correlate of labor market success, and school attendance should be given priority in any job creation program. If attractive jobs are to be offered this age group, they should be tied to school retention. To be attractive, the jobs should provide useful work experiences, access to training, and openings to new career ladders. Such careers do not need to be within one firm, agency, or occupation, as long as there is the opportunity, over time, to move to something better.

With a little imagination it should be possible to create such jobs in the public sector. The real challenge appears to be in the private sector, where youth jobs are not usually distinguished by their meaningfulness. Care must be taken that subsidized private jobs are a step upward in long term career development, not just cheap labor or a holding action. Cooperative work-education programs may be a partial answer. Public authority should take some continuing responsibility for the meaningfulness and long term value of any employment experience provided through subsidization of private employment. Such monitoring can occur at the point of job selection without interfering with the conduct of the employer's business.

Education and Training. While job creation is a critical element in the set of labor market policies needed for response to the youth employment dilemma, there is also a need for policies concerned with basic skill development and job readiness. In the late 1960s, the literature of economics was replete with studies demonstrating the limited value of education and training for labor market assimilation. Emphasis was placed instead upon the structure of labor markets and access to career ladders leading to jobs in high-wage, stable occupations. Blacks and women, it was said, did not have access to these jobs in proportion to their numbers. Moreover, education and training mattered little in opening the door to these jobs.

While not discounting this thesis totally, the economic literature of the 1970s has been more positive, citing increasing returns to education and training for young blacks and women. The results of this study support the recent literature. Education and training, as measured in this study, are closely correlated with the earnings and employment experience of young men and young women, black and white. The results support a continued emphasis upon these policies in responding to youth unemployment. Their importance is highlighted by awareness of the economy's changing occupational structure and skill needs and the effect of education and training investments during youth upon subsequent investment and earnings.

136

Other studies have shown, for example, that investment in education and training during youth is closely correlated with subsequent investment over the life cycle. Those who invest early, continue to invest later. Thus, part of the economic returns to education and training during youth is realized through access to subsequent education and training opportunities. Not only is this important to early labor market success, but also to avoidance of later economic and social problems associated with declining investment and ensuing skill obsolescence with age. For all of these reasons, it makes good economic sense to emphasize education and training during youth. This is not to argue that education and training programs do not need improvement. In most cases they do. The problems of education in central cities are only one case in point. What is argued is that these programs, however imperfect, *do* work and that the rush to judgment in the late 1960s was premature.

In developing skills, formal schooling provides an important foundation on which to build. Job-specific skills, however, may require additional training outside formal education. For some, this training may offer a second chance to develop skills normally acquired within the formal education system. The results of this study show that when job-specific skills are developed, as measured by training used on the job, the effect upon earnings and employment is substantial, with the effect greater for blacks than whites. In this context training can be considered as another form of public subsidy akin to that of job creation. In most cases the two represent complementary forms of investment in youth employability. Job-specific training, when accompanied by stipends, can reduce short term economic hardship for the trainee while also increasing his or her long term employability and earnings. These results, of course, may vary from program to program and should be evaluated accordingly.

The training needs of individuals as well as the resources available from location to location will vary substantially, suggesting the need for a mix of delivery systems. This philosophy is already present within the Comprehensive Employment and Training Act with its emphasis on state and local planning. In some cases, where the background and environment of the individual hinder development or the lack of jobs and training resources precludes access to experience and training, residential training centers, as found in the Job Corps, will be needed. In other cases, training can be provided through existing institutions or on the job. Combinations of these approaches will sometimes be needed.

The volunteer armed forces offers another important source of training for youth. The military currently absorbs about one-third of all noncollege-bound male youths. For some, the military becomes a career, but for the majority it offers an aging vat, a means of acquiring experience and training before returning to the civilian sector. In contrast to other training programs, the military, which is generally underemployed in peacetime, offers a unique opportunity for low-cost expansion of the nation's training resources. The military can promise jobs and skills that are compatible with civilian needs. By doing so it could increase its capacity to compete with this sector for personnel, more fully utilize its resources in a period of peacetime, and increase the employability of youths who elect to return to civilian life.

Along with jobs, education, and training, there is a need for better bridges between school and work. The substitution of better counseling and job orientation in career education is potentially an important alternative to youth turnover and unemployment and the "musical chairs" approach to career development. The results of this study, using a measure of labor market knowledge, support this conclusion. Not only do youths need career education to develop realistic expectations concerning the world of work, but also to develop knowledge of how labor markets work, of alternative career paths, and of the steps necessary to move along a given path. No one is born knowing how to search for a job; it is a skill that needs to be taught like most other skills.

In addition to the need for career education in building better bridges between school and work is the need for better job placement. The tendency of youths not to use the federal-state employment service for this purpose, as shown in Chapter Three, deserves further study. It may be based on the belief that most job openings go to friends and relatives of managers and employees and to "gate" applicants. How to get more youths into these effective job search streams is worthy of study.

Market Intervention. While demonstrating the need for jobs, education, and training in response to youth unemployment, the study also highlights the importance of market interventionist policies and their role, positive and negative, in the youth employment problem. For example, this study raises several important questions concerning the need for aggressive policies of equal employment opportunity and affirmative action. Why is it that youths appear to follow different career paths by race and sex, with these differences emerging early in the labor market experience? What underlies the differences in occupational mobility found among young blacks and whites? What role does overt labor market discrimination play in these differences? There are no hard answers to these questions provided here, but the weight of the evidence argues for continued emphasis upon policies of equal employment opportunity and affirmative action. Interventionist policies like these are an important complement to other policies concerned with job creation and skill development.

Whereas, government policies of equal employment opportunity and affirmative action can play a positive role in addressing some of the underlying structural aspects of youth employment and earnings experiences, other interventionist policies can play a negative role. Perhaps the most often debated of these is the minimum wage. This study provides no direct evidence of the impact of minimum wages upon youth employment, pro or con. What it does provide is a better understanding of the importance of work experience to youths in terms of their future employability and earnings. Any interventionist policy which serves to destroy jobs for youths should be examined closely in light of this evidence.

Although the debate continues, the consensus among academics and others, with notable exceptions in the labor movement, is that minimum wages contribute to the decline of low-skill jobs where youths are heavily clustered. At issue is the magnitude of this decline. In Congressional debate over the 1977 amendments to the Fair Labor Standards Act, raising the minimum wage from $2.30 to $2.65 per hour, estimates of the jobs to be destroyed by this increase ranged from 90 thousand to 900 thousand. With 800 thousand jobs needed for out-of-school youths, the importance of this increase in the minimum wage clearly depends upon whose estimate is correct.

The basis for a minimum wage may be one of equity, providing a minimum standard of living to the employed poor. Or, alternatively, it may represent a means to protect the economic interest of those without power at the bargaining table. If the minimum wage is to be continued, for these or other reasons, more should be known about its job displacement effect. To the extent this effect for youths is significant, it should be considered in job creation efforts. The displacement effect of a minimum wage, however, may not be as great as some have suggested, given growth of the nation's income transfer system. For many, this system provides an alternative to working for low wages. The potential effect upon labor supply may, in itself, drive up wages in low-skill work, leading to job displacement. The proposals described above for job creation in the private sector, nevertheless, provide one means to offset the job displacement effect of a minimum wage by subsidizing youth wages.

Another proposal often offered involves a youth minimum wage differential. As proposed, the youth minimum wage differential would apply to all youths below a given age. The simplicity of this approach is attractive in that it requires little additional administrative overhead beyond that already present in enforcing the Fair Labor Standards Act. No eligibility criteria would have to be developed or administered. Yet, in its simplicity there are problems. For example, it does not provide a means for targeting jobs where they are needed most. In creating a lower wage for youth, it may increase unemployment among other groups such as women, minorities, and older workers for whom youths are substituted. It may even lead to the substitution of teenagers for young adults if, for example, the youth differential is restricted to the younger group. Substitution of youths for other workers may also occur under wage subsidy proposals, of course, but the scope of substitution under well-targeted wage subsidy proposals would not be as great as that under a minimum wage differential applied to all youths. Not only could wage subsidies be targeted to individuals, but also, if possible, to certain occupations, encouraging the movement of youths into growth occupations as needed.

The lessons for public policy drawn from this study have emphasized job creation and skill development. As policies, these are not new. What is new is the evidence supporting them. For perhaps the first time, evidence has been provided which links the early employment experience of out-of-school youths to their subsequent employability and earnings. As such, this adds new emphasis and urgency to youth job creation efforts. The importance of education and training to the employment and earnings of young men and women, black and white, supports the findings of other studies in the 1970s. Together, these policies offer constructive solutions for the youth employment challenge.

Additional Research Needs

In developing effective programs and policies from the lessons above, additional research will be needed. Among the issues to be considered is that of the youth labor supply response under a program of guaranteed jobs. How many youths would enter the labor market under such a program and under what terms? How employable will these youths be and what training will have to be provided? In creating jobs for youths in the private sector, one must be concerned about where the jobs would be located in relation to the universe of need.

Looking at the effect of youth wage subsidies upon other labor force groups, with whom are youths competing for jobs? To what extent are youths substitutes for these groups and to what extent would substitution occur under alternative subsidy levels? Where minimum wages are concerned, can the job displacement effect of recent changes be more accurately determined? In building better bridges between school and work, can a program of career education reduce youth turnover and unemployment? What factors underlie youths' underutilization of the federal-state employment service? What factors influence the choice of occupation and industry among new labor force entrants by race and sex?

Under what incentive structure can youth dropouts be encouraged to complete a secondary education? What factors are known to influence the dropout decision? Among central city youths, what is the scope of extralegal market activities, what are their return in income and peer respect, and how do these influence education and labor force activity? What role does alienation play in the employability of central city youths and those elsewhere? What is the relationship of youth unemployment to juvenile delinquency? While not representing an exhaustive list of youth research needs, these represent some of the more important issues to be resolved in further development of a policy agenda for youth employment.

A Sense of Priority

Youth unemployment, like the poor, will always be with us. In most cases, inexperienced new entrants will be at a competitive disadvantage. Some threshing around at the labor market entrance will always be one of the more effective forms of career exploration. For in-school youths from families of middle and higher income there may be more gained than lost. But for out-of-school youths and especially for the minority, the poor, and the female, the long lasting economic and social costs have been demonstrated. Demographic trends promise some improvement, but the outlook justifies the current priority placed upon the search for solutions. The appeal of this study is for long term solutions consistent with the labor market realities revealed by analysis of available data.

BIBLIOGRAPHY

Adams, Arvil V., and Nestel, Gilbert. "Interregional Migration, Education, and Poverty in the Urban Ghetto: Another Look at Black-White Earnings Differentials." *Review of Economics and Statistics,* May 1976, pp. 156-166.

Altman, Stephen. "Sputnik Put School and Training in New Orbit." *Worklife,* November 1976.

Anderson, Bernard. "Youth Unemployment Problems in the Inner City." In Congressional Budget Office, *The Teenage Unemployment Problem: What Are the Options.* Washington, D.C.: U.S. Government Printing Office, 1976.

Barret, Nancy S., and Mergenston, Richard D. "Why Do Blacks and Women Have High Unemployment Rates?" *Journal of Human Resources,* Fall 1974, pp. 462-465.

Becker, Gary S. *Human Capital: A Theoretical and Empirical Analysis with Special Reference to Education.* New York: National Bureau of Economic Research, 1964.

Becnel, Barbara. "Profiling the Black Worker, 1976." *AFL-CIO American Federationist,* July 1976, pp. 11-20.

Berger, Brigette. "People Work: The Youth Culture and the Labor Market." *The Public Interest,* Spring 1974, pp. 55-66.

Bernert, Eleanor. *America's Children.* New York: John Wiley and Sons, 1958.

Beugirman, Michael, and Cooper, Nicholas C. "Working Youths and Select Findings from an Explanatory Study." *Journal of Youth and Adolescence,* March 1974, pp. 7-16.

Bobrow, Sue. *Reasonable Expectations: Limits on the Promise of Community Councils.* Santa Monica, Calif.: Rand Corporation, 1976.

Bowen, William G., and Finegan, T. Aldrich. "Labor Force Participation and Unemployment." *Employment Policy and the Labor Market.* Edited by Arthur M. Ross. Berkeley, Calif.: University of California Press, 1965.

143

Brimmer, Andrew. *The Economic Position of Black Americans: 1976.* Special Report No. 9, National Commission for Manpower Policy. Washington, D.C.: U.S. Government Printing Office, 1976.

Bullock, Paul. *Youth Labor Market Information Study.* Los Angeles, Calif.: Institute of Industrial Relations, University of California, January 1972.

Burdetsky, Ben. "Troubled Transition: From School to Work." *Worklife,* November 1976.

Cain, Glen G. "The Challenge of Segmented Labor Market Theories to Orthodox Theory: A Survey." *Journal of Economic Literature,* December 1976, pp. 1215-1257.

Caplan, Nathan. *Competency Among Hard-to-Employ Youths.* Washington, D.C.: U.S. Government Printing Office, June 1973.

Coleman, James. *Youth, Transition to Adulthood.* Chicago: University of Chicago Press, 1974.

Coleman, James. "Equal Schools or Equal Students." *The Public Interest,* Summer 1966, pp. 70-75.

Corcoran, Mary; Jencks, Christopher; and Olneck, Michael. "The Effects of Family Background on Earnings." *American Economic Review,* May 1976, pp. 430-435.

Cottereill, Phillip, and Wadych, Walter. "Teenagers and the Minimum Wage in Retail Trade." *Journal of Human Resources,* Winter 1976, pp. 69-85.

Dean, A. J. H. "Unemployment Among School Leavers: An Analysis of the Problem." *National Institute Economic Review,* November 1976, pp. 63-68.

Doeringer, Peter B. *Programs to Employ the Disadvantaged.* Englewood Cliffs, N.J.: Prentice-Hall, Inc., 1969.

Doeringer, Peter B., and Piore, Michael. *Internal Labor Markets and Manpower Analysis.* Lexington, Mass.: D. C. Heath, 1971.

Duncan, Otis Dudley. "A Socioeconomic Index for All Occupations." Albert Reiss, *et al., Occupations and Social Status.* New York: Free Press of Glencoe, 1961.

Edwards, Linda N. "School Retention of Teenagers over the Business Cycle." *Journal of Human Resources,* Spring 1976, pp. 200-208.

Feldstein, Martin S. "Lowering the Permanent Rate of Unemployment: A Study." Joint Economic Committee Printing, 93rd Congress, 1st Session, September 18, 1973.

Feldstein, Martin S. "The Economics of the New Unemployment." *The Public Interest,* Fall 1973, pp. 3-42.

Fisher, Alan. "The Problem of Teenage Unemployment." Ph.D. dissertation, University of California, 1973.

Folk, Hugh. "The Problem of Youth Unemployment." *The Transition from School to Work.* Princeton, N.J.: Princeton University Press, 1968, pp. 76-107.

Freedman, Marcia. "Appendix: An Outline of the Issues and Policy Perspectives." *From School to Work: Improving the Transition.* National Commission on Manpower Policy. Washington, D.C.: U.S. Government Printing Office, 1976, pp. 297-304.

Freedman, Marcia. "The Youth Labor Market." *From School to Work: Improving the Transition.* National Commission on Manpower Policy. Washington, D.C.: U.S. Government Printing Office, 1976, pp. 21-36.

Freeman, Richard. "Teenage Unemployment: Can Reallocating Educational Expenditures Help?" *The Teenage Unemployment Problem.* Congressional Budget Office Report, October 1976.

Friedlander, Stanley L. *Unemployment in the Urban Core: An Analysis of Thirty Cities with Policy.* New York: Praeger Publishers, Inc., 1972.

Fullerton, Howard, Jr., and Flaim, Paul O. "New Labor Force Projections to 1990." *Monthly Labor Review,* December 1976, pp. 3-13.

Gallaway, Lowell E. "Unemployment Levels Among Non-White Teenagers." *Journal of Business,* July 1969, pp. 265-276.

Goldstein, Bernard. *Low Income Youth in Urban Areas.* New York: Holt, Reinhart, and Winston, 1967.

Gordon, David M. *Theories of Poverty and Underemployment.* Lexington, Mass.: D. C. Heath, 1972.

145

Gramlich, Edward M. "Impact of Minimum Wages on Other Wages, Employment, and Family Incomes." *Brookings Papers on Economic Activity,* 2, 1976, pp. 409-461.

Gramlich, Edward M. "The Distributional Effects of Higher Unemployment." *Brookings Papers on Economic Activity,* 2, 1974, pp. 293-336.

Grasso, John. "Dimensions of Youth Unemployment." *Career Thresholds.* Columbus, Ohio: Center for Human Resource Research, Ohio State University, 1977.

Gurin, Gerald. *Inner-City Negro Youth in a Job Training Project.* Ann Arbor, Mich.: Institute for Social Research, University of Michigan, 1968.

Guzzardidi, Walter. "How to Deal with the 'New Unemployment'." *Fortune,* October 1976, pp. 132-135, 208-216.

Hall, Robert E., and Kasten, Richard A. "Occupational Mobility and the Distribution of Occupational Success Among Young Men." *American Economic Review,* May 1976, pp. 309-315.

Hanoch, Giora. "An Economic Analysis of Earnings and Schooling." *Journal of Human Resources.* Summer 1967, pp. 310-329.

Harrison, Bennett. "Ghetto Economic Development." *Journal of Economic Literature,* March 1974, pp. 1-37.

Harrison, Bennett. *Education, Training, and the Urban Ghetto.* Baltimore, Md.: Johns Hopkins University Press, 1972.

Harrison, Bennett. "Education and Underemployment in the Urban Ghetto." *American Economic Review,* December 1972, pp. 796-812.

Harrison, Bennett. *Public Employment and Urban Poverty.* Washington, D.C.: The Urban Institute, 1971.

Harrison, Michael. "The Harbor City is the Classroom." *Worklife,* November 1976.

Harwood, Edwin. "Youth Unemployment—A Tale of Two Ghettos." *The Public Interest,* Fall 1969, pp. 78-87.

Hedges, Janice. "Youth Unemployment in the 1974-75 Recession." *Monthly Labor Review,* January 1976, pp. 49-56.

146

Hill, Russell, and Stafford, Frank. "Allocation of Time to Preschool Children and Educational Opportunity." *Journal of Human Resources,* Summer 1974, pp. 323-431.

Jencks, Christopher, *et al. Inequality: A Reassessment of the Effect of Family and Schooling in America.* New York: Basic Books, 1972.

Johnston, Jerome, and Bachman, Jerald. *The Transition from High School to Work: The Work Attitudes and Early Occupational Experience of Young Men.* Ann Arbor, Mich.: University of Michigan, 1973.

Kalachek, Edward. "The Changing Economic Status of the Young." *Journal of Youth and Adolescence.* June 1973, 125-132.

Kalachek, Edward. *The Youth Labor Market.* Policy papers in Human Resources and Industrial Relations No. 12. Ann Arbor, Mich.: The Institute of Labor and Industrial Relations, University of Michigan and Wayne State University, 1969.

Kalachek, Edward. "Determinants of Teen Age Unemployment." *Journal of Human Resources,* Winter 1969, pp. 3-21.

King, Christopher T. "The Unemployment Impact of the Vietnam War." Ph.D. dissertation, Michigan State University, 1976.

Kohen, Andrew. "Antecedents and Consequences of Occupational Mobility." *Career Thresholds,* Volume 6. Washington, D.C.: U.S. Department of Labor, Employment and Training Administration, 1977.

Kohen, Andrew. *Determinants of Early Labor Market Success Among Young Men: Race, Ability, Quantity and Quality of Schooling.* Columbus, Ohio: Center for Human Resources Research, 1973.

Korbel, John. "Labor Force Entry and Attachment of Young People." *Journal of American Statistical Association,* March 1966, pp. 117-127.

Leigh, Duane E. "The Occupational Mobility of Young Men, 1965-1970." *Industrial and Labor Relations Review,* October 1976, pp. 68-78.

Leigh, Duane E. "Labor Force Participation of Male Youth Living in Low Income Urban Areas." *Industrial and Labor Relations Review,* January 1974, pp. 242-248.

147

Levitan, Sar A. "Coping with Teenage Unemployment." Congressional Budget Office, *The Teenage Unemployment Problem: What Are the Options?* Washington, D.C.: U.S. Government Printing Office, 1976.

Levitan, Sar A., and Mangum, Garth L. *Federal Work and Training Programs in the Sixties.* Ann Arbor, Mich.: Institute of Labor and Industrial Relations, University of Michigan, 1969.

Levitan, Sar A.; Mangum, Garth L.; and Taggart, Robert. *Economic Opportunity in the Ghetto: The Partnership of Government and Business.* Baltimore, Md.: Johns Hopkins University Press, 1970.

Levitan, Sar A.; Johnston, William B.; and Taggart, Robert, *Minorities in the United States: Problems, Progress, and Prospects.* Washington, D.C.: Public Affairs Press, 1975.

Levitan, Sar A.; Johnston, William B.; and Taggart, Robert. *Still A Dream: The Changing Status of Blacks Since 1960.* Cambridge, Mass.: Harvard University Press, 1975.

Levitan, Sar A.; Rein, Martin; and Marwick, David. *Work and Welfare Go Together.* Baltimore, Md.: Johns Hopkins University Press, 1972.

Levitan, Sar A., and Taggart, Robert. *The Promise of Greatness.* Cambridge, Mass.: Harvard University Press, 1976.

Levitan, Sar A., and Taggart, Robert. *The Job Corps: A Social Experiment That Works.* Baltimore, Md.: Johns Hopkins University Press, 1975.

Levitan, Sar A., and Taggart, Robert. "Background Papers on Job Crisis for Black Youth." Twentieth Century Fund Task Force on Employment Problems of Black Youth. *The Job Crisis for Black Youth.* New York: Praeger Publishers, Inc., 1971.

Mangum, Garth L. *Employability, Employment, and Income: A Reassessment of Manpower Policy.* Salt Lake City, Utah: Olympus Publishing Co., 1976.

Mangum, Garth L., and Seninger, Stephen F. *Coming of Age in the Ghetto: The Dilemma of Ghetto Youth Unemployment.* Report submitted to Ford Foundation, December 1977.

Mangum, Garth L., and Walsh, John. *A Decade of Manpower Development and Training.* Salt Lake City, Utah: Olympus Publishing Co., 1973.

Marans, Robert W.; Druver, B. L.; and Scott, John C. *Youth and the Environment: An Evaluation of the 1971 Youth Conservation Corps.* Ann Arbor, Mich.: Institute for Social Research, 1972.

National Child Labor Committee. *Rite of Passage: The Crisis of Youth's Transition from School to Work.* Washington, D.C.: U.S. Government Printing Office, 1976.

National Commission for Manpower Policy. *The Challenge of Rising Unemployment.* Interim Report to the Congress. Washington, D.C.: U.S. Government Printing Office, 1975.

National Commission for Manpower Policy. *The Economic Position of Black Americans: 1976.* Washington, D.C.: U.S. Government Printing Office, 1976.

National Commission on Manpower Policy. *From School to Work.* Washington, D.C.: U.S. Government Printing Office, 1976.

National Council on Crime and Delinquency. *Training for New Careers—The Community Apprentice Program.* Washington, D.C.: Howard University Press, no date.

National Council on Crime and Delinquency. *Training for New Careers—The Opportunity Apprentice Program.* Washington, D.C.: Howard University Press, no date.

New York City Youth Board. *Youth in New York City: Out of School and Out of Work.* Report of the Mayor's Committee on Youth and Work, December 1965.

Ornstein, Michael D. *Entry Into the American Labor Force.* Toronto: York University Press, 1976.

Osterman, Paul. *The Structure of the Labor Market for Young Men.* Mimeographed manuscript, 1977.

Parnes, Herbert S. *The National Longitudinal Surveys.* Columbus, Ohio: Center for Human Resources, 1974.

Parnes, Herbert S., and Kohen, Andrew. "Labor Market Experience of Noncollege Youth: A Longitudinal Analysis." *From School to Work: Improving the Transition.* National Commission for Manpower Policy. Washington, D.C.: U.S. Government Printing Office, 1976, pp. 57-88.

Parnes, Herbert S., and Kohen, Andrew. "Occupational Information and Labor Market Status: The Case of Young Men." *Journal of Human Resources,* Winter 1975, pp. 44-55.

Perry, George L. "Potential Output and Productivity." *Brookings Papers on Economic Activity,* 1, 1977, pp. 11-60.

Porter, James N. "Race, Socialization, Maturity in Educational Attainment." *American Sociological Review,* June 1974, pp. 303-316.

Price, Hugh B.; Zelinsky, Doris; and Johnston, William B. "An Urban Service Corps for Unemployed Youth." *The Review of Black Political Economy,* Spring 1976, pp. 279-293.

Ragan, James F. "Minimum Wages and the Youth Labor Market." *Review of Economics and Statistics,* May 1977, pp. 129-136.

Rees, Albert, and Schultz, George P. *Workers and Wages in An Urban Labor Market.* Chicago: University of Chicago Press, 1970.

Reubens, Beatrice. "Foreign and American Experience with the Youth Transition." *From School to Work: Improving the Transition.* National Commission on Manpower Policy. Washington, D.C.: U.S. Government Printing Office, 1976, pp. 273-296.

Reubens, Beatrice, "Foreign Experiences." Congressional Budget Office, *The Teenage Unemployment Problem: What Are the Options?* Washington, D.C.: U.S. Government Printing Office, 1976.

Shiskin, Julius. "Employment and Unemployment: The Doughnut or the Hole." *Monthly Labor Review,* February 1976.

Silberman, Charles. "What Hit the Teenagers." *Fortune,* April 1965.

Singell, L. D. "Economic Opportunity and Juvenile Delinquency—A Case Study of the Detroit Juvenile Labor Market." Ph.D. dissertation, University of Michigan, 1965.

Smith, Ralph. "The Teenage Unemployment Problem—How Much Will Macro Policies Matter?" *The Teenage Unemployment Problem: What Are the Options?* Washington, D.C.: U.S. Government Printing Office, 1976.

Staples, Robert. "To Be Young, Black, and Oppressed." *Black Scholar,* July 1976, pp. 39-47.

Stephenson, Stanley P. "The Economics of Youth Job Search Behavior." *Review of Economic and Statistics,* February 1976, pp. 104-116.

Stevenson, Gelvin. "Determinants of the Occupational Employment of Black and White Male Teenagers." Ph.D. dissertation, Washington University, 1973.

Super, Donald E., and Overstreet, Phoebe L. *The Vocational Maturity of Ninth-Grade Boys.* New York: Columbia University, 1960.

Taubman, Paul. "Earnings, Education, Genetics, and Environment." *Journal of Human Resources,* Fall 1976, pp. 447-461.

Tella, Alfred. "Hidden Unemployment 1953-62—A Quantitative Analysis by Age and Sex: Comments." *American Economic Review,* December 1966, pp. 1235-1240.

Tella, Alfred. "Labor Force Sensitivity to Employment by Age and Sex." *Industrial Relations,* February 1965, pp. 69-83.

Thurow, Lester. *Poverty and Discrimination.* Washington, D.C.: The Brookings Institution, 1969.

U.S. Department of Labor. *Groups with Historically High Incidence of Unemployment.* Washington, D.C.: Employment Standards Administration, July 1977.

U.S. Department of Labor. *1977 Employment and Training Report of the President.* Washington, D.C.: U.S. Government Printing Office, 1977.

U.S. Department of Labor. *Improving Employment Opportunities for Female Black Teenagers in New York City.* Research and Development, Monograph No. 47, 1977.

U.S. Department of Labor, Bureau of Labor Statistics. *Students, Graduates, and Dropouts in the Labor Market, October 1975.* Special Labor Force Report No. 191. Washington, D.C.: U.S. Government Printing Office, 1976.

U.S. Department of Labor. *Employment in Perspective: Summer Job Situation for Youth, 1976.* Washington, D.C.: U.S. Government Printing Office, 1976.

U.S. Department of Labor. *Youth and the Meaning of Work.* Manpower Research Monograph No. 32. Washington, D.C.: U.S. Government Printing Office, 1974.

Wallace, P. A. *Pathways to Work—Unemployment Among Black Teenage Females.* Lexington, Mass.: Heath Lexington Books, 1974.

Walther, Regis H., and Magnusson, Margaret L. "A Longitudinal Study of Selected Out of School NYC-2 Programs in Four Cities." Manpower Administration, final report. Washington, D.C.: U.S. Government Printing Office, 1975.

Weiss, Leonard, and Williamson, J. G. "Black Education, Earnings, and Interregional Migration: Some New Evidence." *American Economic Review,* June 1972, pp. 372-383.

Welch, Finis. "Black-White Differences in Return to Schooling." *American Economic Review,* December 1973, pp. 893-907.

Westcott, Diane. "The Nation's Youth: An Employment Perspective." *Worklife,* June 1977, pp. 13-19.

Westcott, Diane. "Youth in the Labor Force: An Area Study." *Monthly Labor Review,* July 1976, pp. 3-9.

Winter, Elmer. "The Businessman's Role in Closing the Gap Between Education and the Job." *The Transition from School to Work.* Princeton, N.J.: Princeton University Press, 1968.

Zimpel, Lloyd. *The Disadvantaged Worker.* Reading, Mass.: Addison-Wesley Publishing Co., 1971.

Zschock, Dieter. "Black Youths in Suburbia." *Urban Affairs Quarterly,* September 1971, pp. 61-74.